THE SPELLMOUNT
LONDON
IN THE
SECOND WORLD WAR

THE SPELLMOUNT GUIDE TO
LONDON
IN THE
SECOND WORLD WAR

JAMES BEARDON

For my dad

Cover Images: *Front*: Bank Underground station following bombing (© TfL from the London Transport Museum) and today (author). *Back*: Balham High Road then (© TfL from the London Transport Museum) and now (author).

First published 2013
by Spellmount, an imprint of The History Press
The Mill, Brimscombe Port
Stroud, Gloucestershire, GL5 2QG
www.thehistorypress.co.uk

British Library Cataloguing in Publication Data.
A catalogue record for this book is available from the British Library.

ISBN 978 0 7524 9349 7

Typesetting and origination by The History Press
Printed in Great Britain

CONTENTS

AUTHOR'S NOTE & ACKNOWLEDGEMENTS

This book came about over many long commutes up to London with too much time to think and lunchtime walks around a city where there is always something new, or in this case old, to find. In this Spellmount guidebook I have tried to pick out the most interesting and relevant buildings and places in London that can be visited today, where an event relating to the Second World War took place. What I hope to convey is the sense of how Londoners, and the Allied nations, joined together to fight for their very survival.

This book would never have happened without the help, guidance and support of so many people along the way. First, I must mention Matt (and his bottle of Glenfiddich). Without either, this project would still be languishing; thanks for the encouragement you gave me when I first mentioned this idea and making me believe it was a worthy one.

I must also thank Robert, my agent, for taking this one on, for clearly it would not have happened without your support; Shaun and Lauren at The History Press, always at the end of an email to answer my more obscure questions; Paul, for your willingness to listen to my latest updates and gems of knowledge over many bike rides but, most of all, for the honest opinion of the book, it is without doubt better for it. Mum, thanks for the enthusiastic support you have given me throughout this project. I would also like to thank the London Transport Museum who allowed me to use photographs from their archive, and in particular Anna Renton.

Last, but by no means least, my thanks to the three girls in my life: my wife Sarah, who has been there for me and helped me overcome every problem, both great and small, I could not have done this, or much, without you. And of course my daughters, Emma and Sophie – you make it all worthwhile.

For the many others who have been involved in the making of this book, I thank you; the improvements are yours while the errors are all mine.

www.james.beardon.co.uk

LIST OF ABBREVIATIONS & TERMS

AA	Anti-Aircraft
Abwehr	German secret intelligence organisation
ARP	Air-raid Precaution
BBC	British Broadcasting Corporation
BEF	British Expeditionary Force, which was sent to France immediately after the invasion of Poland
BT	British Telecom
'C'	Head of SIS
CBS	American news service and radio broadcasting organisation
CCFL	Caisse Centrale de la France Libre, the bank of the Free French
CIA	Central Intelligence Agency, the modern intelligence organisation whose origins lie in the Second World War as the OSS
CIGS	Chief of the Imperial General Staff
CSDIC	Combined Services Detailed Interrogation Centre
DLR	Docklands Light Railway
DNI	Director Naval Intelligence
DSO	Distinguished Service Order, a medal for valour
Enigma	German coding machine that was used to send secret messages whose code was supposed to be unbreakable
ETOUSA	European Theatre of Operation, United States Army
ENSA	Entertainments National Service Association
FANY	First Aid Nursing Yeomanry
FBI	Federal Bureau of Investigation
F-S	Fairbairn Sykes (usually associated with their fighting knife)
GC&CS	Government Code & Cypher School, the organisation run from Bletchley Park that broke the German Enigma code
IAU	Intelligence Assault Unit
ISRB	Inter Services Research Bureau, a cover name for SOE
IS9(d)	Intelligence School Number 9, which was part of MI9

JIC	Joint Intelligence Committee, who oversee the work of the secret services
Kriegsmarine	German 'war' navy
LT	London Transport
LTPB	London Transport Passenger Board
MC	Military Cross, a medal for valour only subordinate to the Victoria Cross
Met	Metropolitan Police Force
MI5	Commonly used name for the Security Service responsible for homeland security such as penetrating British-based subversive organisations and counter-espionage work
MI6	Common name for the Secret Intelligence Service
MI9	Wartime escape and evasion organisation
MoD	Ministry of Defence, responsible for the running of the Army, Navy and Air Force
MP	Member of Parliament
NID	Naval Intelligence Department
NPO	New Public Offices, the building under which the War Rooms can be found and which was converted into the Number 10 Annex
OSS	Office of Strategic Studies, an American organisation roughly equivalent to SIS and the forerunner of the CIA
PLA	Port of London Authority
PM	Prime Minister
POW	Prisoner of war
RAF	Royal Air Force
RCAF	Royal Canadian Air Force
RN	Royal Navy
RTR	Royal Tank Regiment
SAS	Special Air Service
SHAEF	Supreme Headquarters of the Allied Expeditionary Force, the overall name given to Eisenhower's command for the D-Day landings
SIGSALY	American voice encryption technology
SIS	Secret Intelligence Service, colloquially known as MI6, responsible for intelligence gathering abroad
SOE	Special Operations Executive, the resistance and sabotage organisation set up during the early phases of the war
VE Day	Victory in Europe day
WAAF	Women's Auxiliary Air Force
WAPC	Women's Auxiliary Police Corps
WOKs	Worked Out Keys, a new coding method devised by Leo Marks
WVS	Women's Voluntary Service
XX Committee	The double cross system run by the Security Service where German agents were turned to feed false information to the Abwehr

ABOUT THE GUIDEBOOK

In the mid- to late 1930s, immense changes were in motion around the world as political views and social divides shifted. Colonies around the globe ensured Britain maintained her global reach and influence, with politicians giving little consideration to the idea that this status quo could ever be challenged. France, comforted by the Maginot Line and what proved to be delusional self-belief in its armed forces, continued to deem itself safe from any aggressor. On the other side of the Atlantic, America continued to view European troubles with some disdain, firmly believing they should be resolved by Europeans and would not impact on America in any way. Fascism was in the ascendency in Germany as National Socialism took hold. Hitler had designs on the resources and land of neighbouring countries as he planned the expansion of Germany's borders. The populations of those countries, in many cases, were considered an inconvenience to be dispassionately driven out. And, all the while, he continued to brood on the injustice handed out at Versailles. Meanwhile, Stalin's communist regime's iron grip grew ever tighter around the Russian people, and he too began looking east and west. Further afield, Japanese eyes were firmly locked on lands they could capture, with China, the Philippines and British colonies high on their agenda.

Hitler's first moves to reclaim the Ruhr and to bring Austria into the Reich brought nothing but appeasement from Chamberlain and other European leaders. With no decisive action taken against him, Hitler became more audacious and his next success was to surprise even him. The British and French, in an effort to avoid war at all costs, sacrificed Czechoslovakia with the Munich Agreement. Any remaining hopes of 'peace in our time' were firmly crushed when Poland was invaded in the early hours of 1 September 1939. As the Polish Army and its population were brutally slaughtered, Britain and France declared war but did, and could do, nothing to prevent Poland's rapid demise.

From 3 September 1939, Great Britain moved closer to all-out war. While the phoney war did little to persuade the population that Britain was truly at war, London was changing. Little by little, politicians and military leaders began preparing for the inevitable confrontation. The War Office expanded into nearby hotels; trenches were dug in London's parks as air-raid shelters and sandbags were filled to protect buildings. London was to be the centre of Britain's war effort and it was moving to a war footing.

In May 1940 the Nazis were once again on the offensive and this time they were not to be stopped until they had conquered most of mainland Europe. Defeat was followed by catastrophe for the Allied armies as the French collapsed and the Belgians capitulated. There was the 'miracle of Dunkirk' which saw much of the British Army escape back to the UK alongside those French forces that refused to accept defeat. With the soldiers came European politicians and royalty, exiled from their homelands until such time as they might return. By now the people of Britain knew war was upon them as the coast, countryside and cities were fortified to repel the anticipated invaders. And so it was that London became the centre of the lone resistance to the Nazis in Europe.

Defiantly, Churchill declared that Britain would hold firm despite the continued reverses experienced by British forces and the ferocity of the Blitz. All the while London and its inhabitants continued to evolve; American reporters arrived to witness the bombing while hotels tried to surpass each other with the most luxurious air-raid shelters. The Special Operations Executive (SOE) was formed to take the fight back to the Germans, expanding to take over buildings across the capital.

The pre-emptive strike at Pearl Harbor brought the USA into the war and the American military to London, which had now become the multinational headquarters of the free forces arrayed against Hitler. As their numbers swelled, Grosvenor Square became 'Little America' and then 'Eisenhoplatz'. D-Day saw this vast force cross the Channel to launch the offensive that would lead to ultimate victory over the Nazis.

The events that made up those six years of conflict were to change the world forever and London was at the centre of those terrible years. As it simultaneously became both the front line and the command centre of Allied operations against the Axis nations, the city was adapted. The breadth, scale and speed of the city's transformation to meet the needs of the moment is unparalleled in London's history.

Set against this background, this book will guide the reader, as a virtual tourist, around London as it was during the war years from 1939 to 1945, showing how the capital changed. Buildings that had a specific wartime use or have a link to an important event that occurred during the war are revealed, along with the often-secret activities, known only to a select few at the time, of the organisations that occupied them. Buildings used as air-raid shelters, iconic buildings damaged by enemy bombing and how London itself changed will all be brought to life. Some buildings have, in later years, been marked by blue or green plaques to mark these historic events and are displayed prominently.

Additionally, since the end of the war, many of its notable participants have been honoured with statues and memorials, from individual men such as Winston Churchill and Viscount Slim to groups of people such as the London fire fighters. An additional section marks the locations of these memorials, with another detailing museums relating to the Second World War that can be found in London.

Each point of interest has a history of its link to the Second World War, such as the organisation that used a building, how a building was transformed for wartime use, an event that occurred at a certain location or the role a person or group of people honoured played during those years.

Finally, suggested walks and cycle tours (which can be carried out using the London Cycle Hire Scheme bikes) can take the modern-day tourist around London and the many Second World War features that still remain.

Using the Guidebook

This book is intended to guide the reader around the sites and sights of Second World War London. The book can be used to locate and visit all the sites featured, but will be of equal interest to the armchair reader building up an image of how London was during the Second World War.

The book itself focuses on central London, roughly covering the boroughs of Kensington and Chelsea across to Tower Hamlets north of the Thames and Wandsworth, Lambeth and Southwark to the south. Many of the areas described are located in the very heart of London and are within the bounds of the Underground's Circle line. Taking Trafalgar Square as a central point, it is easy to head to the main areas of interest.

Additional chapters cover sites of interest related to the London Underground, memorials and museums linked to the Second World War. There are also a range of suggested walking and cycling routes which take the reader around some of the locations mentioned in the book. The cycling routes have been designed to be carried out using the convenient London Cycle Hire Scheme.

If the building that was present during the war no long exists or the site of interest has no actual address (such as a monument), then details are given of how to find the location of the building that would have stood there during the war or how to find the site of interest.

Each map shows the location of each entry as well as showing nearby tube stations and London Cycle Hire bike racks (please refer to Travel and Guided

Routes for additional information on using the London Cycle Hire Scheme and general information on travel around London).
Example entry:

a **Secret Intelligence Service Headquarters**
b 54 BROADWAY

c **Tube**: St James's Park
d **Barclays Cycle Hire**: Abbey Orchard Street, Westminster

e 54 BROADWAY can be found opposite St James's Park Underground station, and is next door to the Old Star Pub, which was there when SIS moved in. Broadway itself is just south of St James's Park and can be reached by crossing Birdcage Walk and going through one of the passageways into Queen Anne's Gate.

a **(Name of occupants/memorial)**
b (STREET ADDRESS)

c (Nearest Underground station)
d (Most convenient Barclays Cycle Hire bike rack)

e (Information to locate the entry more precisely if possible, as some original buildings have been demolished since the war)

Devastation caused by bombing in Islington.

The Kensington area is centred on Kensington Gardens to the west of Hyde Park. Most of the buildings of interest can be found in Kensington Palace Gardens to the west and then south of the park around Knightsbridge. Wormwood Scrubs Prison lies just outside the borough of Kensington and Chelsea's northern edge.

The whole area has a surprising past, much more than might be expected with the association with high-class shopping. From the abandoned Underground station of Brompton Road to secret training schools and research departments, there is a lot more to Kensington than just its famous department stores and restaurants.

The most well-known area of Kensington is probably Knightsbridge, where Harrods and Harvey Nichols can be found. But, little known at the time, the Secret Intelligence Service (SIS, more commonly known as MI6) had set up training schools for their radio operators and Norwegian agents in the area, while SOE had a photographic section in Trevor Square, a short walk from Harrods. A little further down the Brompton Road, the Underground station by the same name was being used as an anti-aircraft division's control room.

Kensington is able to boast one of the most exclusive streets in London: Kensington Palace Gardens, otherwise known as Palace Green. Several buildings down here are official ambassador residences, most notably those of Norway and Russia, while numbers 6 to 8 had a murkier past as a prisoner interrogation centre where the methods used might perhaps be compared to those of the Gestapo. You may walk up and down this boulevard, but be careful to keep your camera in your bag as there is a strict prohibition on photography. Sections of SOE also found premises in this area, with the camouflage section starting out in the building adjacent to the Natural History Museum, which itself had a demonstration room for dignitaries.

KEY

1. Norwegian Government in Exile
2. Norwegian Ambassador's Residence
3. Residence of the Soviet Union Ambassador to Great Britain
4. The London Cage, MI9 Interrogation Centre
5. SIS, Norwegian Training School
6. SIS, Communications Section VIII
7. SOE Camouflage Section, XVa
8. SOE Photographic and Make-Up Section, XVc
9. SOE Demonstration Room

MI5 HQ, Wormwood Scrubs, 1939–40
DU CANE ROAD

Tube: East Acton
Barclays Cycle Hire: None close

Wormwood Scrubs Prison, with its distinctive gatehouse, can be found on DU CANE ROAD on the south side of Wormwood Scrubs Park, which is on the north-west corner, but just outside of the borough of Kensington and Chelsea. Wormwood Scrubs is still in operation today as a Category B prison, with an operational capacity of nearly 1,300 prisoners.

The Security Service, more commonly known as MI5, has been in existence since 1909, when it was formed as the Secret Service Bureau, which effectively incorporated both MI5 and SIS (usually referred to as MI6). The following year they separated into the two organisations we know today, with MI5 being responsible for all 'home work', including espionage and counter-espionage with Vernon Kell as its chief. SIS was then responsible for all foreign intelligence, with Mansfield Cumming as its chief.

Up to the outbreak of the Second World War, MI5's offices could be found (albeit by very few people) on the top floor of Thames House, Millbank. On 27 August 1939, with the onset of war, Kell, who was still head of MI5 at the age of 66, moved the service from Thames House to Wormwood Scrubs due to an urgent need for more space to carry out wartime work.

By January 1940 the service had grown to 102 officers from just three in July 1939, and continued to grow as the War Cabinet passed an act allowing the internment of anyone believed to be sympathetic to foreign powers. This act resulted in 22,000 Germans and 4,000 Italians being interned, along with 753 members of the British Union of Fascists.

One of the more notable new arrivals at MI5 was Victor Rothschild, who secretly retrieved bomb fuses for research from the Continent and created a counter-sabotage department in one of the cells. Rothschild seemed to enjoy defusing German bombs, such as the one which was hidden in a crate of onions from Spain timed to explode in a British port.

But all was not well with MI5 in its prison home as the Scrubs was not the best working environment. Staff using cells as offices had the alarming possibility of getting locked in due to the obvious lack of a handle on the inside. Meanwhile in official circles, the service was seen as a 'chaotic' organisation that Kell had lost control of. On 10 June 1940, Kell was removed from office (dying in March 1942) to be replaced by Jasper Harker of B Branch (at that time responsible for counter-espionage). Harker did not last very long and, after he had carried out an audit of MI5 which concluded 'that the Service had suffered from poor management and planning which had led to organisational breakdown and confusion', was replaced by Sir David Petrie in 1941.

However, Harker was in charge long enough to oversee the move from prison to palace in October 1940, when the greater part of MI5 was moved from the Scrubs to Blenheim Palace – Churchill's childhood home – after it was concluded that the prison did not offer the protection required. As the Blitz intensified, only the ground-floor offices were thought to be 'reasonably safe', while many of the staff on the upper floors had to vacate their rooms. The Registry, which was the filing system of the organisation where the details of people under investigation were recorded and could be cross-checked, was not as sheltered as it should have been. Unfortunately the decision to locate the Registry in a glass-roofed workshop was proven to be a poor one when a September 1940 bombing raid damaged the prison and much of the Registry was lost to fire or the subsequent water damage caused in dampening the flames.

After the move, some of MI5's staff did remain in London, but not at the Scrubs; they moved into offices at 58 St James Street. Today MI5 can be found back at Thames House at Millbank again.

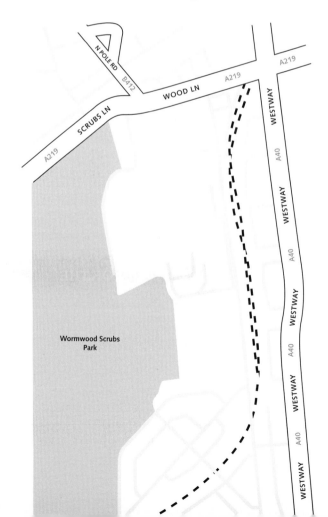

Norwegian Government in Exile

KINGSTON HOUSE NORTH, KENSINGTON ROAD

Tube: Knightsbridge
Barclays Cycle Hire: Exhibition Road, South Kensington

KINGSTON HOUSE NORTH, the home of the Norwegian government in exile after Norway fell to the Nazis, can be found just off Kensington Road on the south side of Hyde Park. The building has a green plaque, unveiled on 27 September 2005, acknowledging its wartime use.

The Scandinavian countries were in a difficult position come the onset of the Second World War. None were in a position to repel any hostile advance for any length of time and therefore had to decide on their political stance with care. Sweden had the closest ties with Germany and managed to remain neutral throughout the war. Meanwhile, Finland had greater issues to consider since it was soon fighting off a Soviet onslaught on its border.

Norway, like Sweden and Denmark, chose to adopt a position of neutrality. While the government's sympathies lay with the Allies, it was made clear by Hitler that Germany would not tolerate a neutral Norway in name that was in fact aiding the Allies. Meanwhile, Britain had secured the charter of much of the Norwegian Merchant Fleet on 11 November 1939, but Norway also signed an agreement to maintain exports at 1938 levels with Germany.

Churchill was soon to become obsessed with Norway and advocated the mining of Norwegian territorial waters to prevent iron ore shipments. This in turn led to a plan to occupy Narvik and other mining districts in Norway.

The green plaque on Kingston House North, marking its use by the Norwegian government.

By April 1940, the situation had developed with both the Germans and British repeatedly breaching Norway's neutrality by entering her waters. Eventually the Allies decided they could wait no longer and put in motion their plan to land troops in Norway.

The embarkation of British, French and Polish troops destined for Narvik coincided with German plans for Norway. Hitler's position at the onset of war was that a neutral Scandinavia was in Germany's best interests, but events changed this view. This was in part due to repeated Allied violations in Norway and the risk posed to Germany of Britain establishing bases in Norway itself. The petitioning from his advisors was also a factor; especially those from the navy who pointed out that the extensive Norwegian coastline offered much greater access for their ships to the North Sea.

In the event, bold German plans to invade were put into action on 8–9 April 1940, when they swiftly overcame the Norwegian forces, which had been in decline since the First World War. The only significant success for Norway came when a coastal fort sank *Blücher*, a recently commissioned troopship, with the loss of over 1,000 German soldiers.

The Norwegian government's reaction was confused and haphazard to say the least. When King Haakon VII was told that the country was at war, his reply was 'with whom?' since it had been considered a distinct possibility that it would be Britain who would be the aggressor. As it transpired, the only significant decision taken was to ask Britain for assistance, which was given forthwith.

No decisive action was taken regarding the mobilisation of the Norwegian armed forces, which was given by mail on 12 April, delaying the formation of their army. However, the Norwegians, supported by Allied forces, fought on for sixty-two days before departing for Britain. The outcome may well have been entirely different had the warning signs of a German invasion been acted on and, once committed, Allied efforts had been better co-ordinated.

On arrival in London, the Norwegian government took out leases on most of the flats in Kingston House North. All aspects of the government were run from these offices, including the Defence Staff, the Central Bank and the Norwegian Broadcasting Corporation. Meanwhile, back in Norway, the Germans were able to look back on a stunning victory, which had by no means been certain. They now controlled Norway via the puppet Quisling government, which secured Norway's iron ore deposits and gave them unhindered access to the North Sea and the Atlantic beyond. A German, rather than British, presence in Norway also removed any chance of Sweden entering the Allied cause and prevented the British from setting up air bases in Norway.

For Britain, the defeat in Norway had one immediate positive effect: the service of the entire Norwegian Merchant Fleet, one of the biggest in the world with a 4.8 million-ton capacity. This fleet was, in part, able to supply Britain throughout the Battle of the Atlantic, but suffered enormous losses in fulfilling this role.

Kingston House North was built in the late 1930s and is now private residential apartments.

Norwegian Ambassador's Residence
10 PALACE GREEN

Tube: Kensington High Street
Barclays Cycle Hire: Kensington Church Street, Kensington

The Norwegian ambassador's official residence can be found at 10 PALACE GREEN (the alternative name for Kensington Palace Gardens), about halfway up on the left-hand side as you head up from Kensington Road. During the war the building was used by King Haakon VII as his official residence while in exile. A prominent blue plaque on the building commemorates this.

The German invasion of Norway was met with confusion and hesitation by the Norwegian government, who had hoped to remain neutral throughout any European conflict. However, Hitler's decision to invade Norway to prevent it falling into British hands quickly ended those hopes.

One of Germany's principal aims was to capture the royal family and Norwegian government in Oslo, but this part of the operation did not go to plan. The German ambassador to Norway, Dr Curt Bräuer, met with the Foreign Minister, Koht, asking for Norway's surrender at about 4.30 a.m. on 9 April 1940. By 7.23 a.m., having declined the surrender, King Haakon VII, Crown Prince Olav, the rest of the royal family and the Cabinet were on a train heading to Hamar, 76 miles north of Oslo. They were soon forced to move on from Hamar when Captain Eberhard Spiller, the German air attaché, organised a company of paratroopers to strike north towards Hamar to capture them. On his arrival at Hamar, he discovered they had already left for Elverum and so continued his journey. Spiller was only stopped by a makeshift force of ninety-three men, including some local gun club members, who ambushed and killed him on the road to Elverum and forced his improvised raiding party back to Oslo.

The evacuation of Allied troops and equipment started in early June 1940, ending any hope of a prolonged Norwegian resistance. The Cabinet held its last meeting on Norwegian soil on 7 June, just before they left for England with the royal family and the diplomatic corps on board the cruiser HMS *Devonshire*.

King Haakon VII landed on British soil in Scotland and headed straight to London, where he received a warm welcome, especially as he was related to the British royal family. King Haakon was married to Princess Maud, who was the youngest daughter of Edward VII and Queen Alexandra, and was King George VI's uncle.

The Norwegian Legation was transformed into his residence, where he presided over weekly Cabinet meetings around a table that is still in use today in the same building. They were to remain in London for five years, until they were able to return to Oslo on 7 June 1945.

No. 10 Palace Green is still in use today as the Norwegian ambassador's official residence.

Residence of the Soviet Union Ambassador to Great Britain
13 KENSINGTON PALACE GARDENS

Tube: Kensington High Street
Barclays Cycle Hire: Kensington Church Street, Kensington

The Soviet Union ambassador's official residence at KENSINGTON PALACE GARDENS can be found a little over halfway up on the right-hand side as you head up from Kensington Road. The house was built in 1852 for the 5th Earl of Harrington and was handed over to the Soviet Union in 1930.

From 1932 to 1943, the ambassador to Great Britain was Ivan Maisky. Maisky had many uncomfortable situations to deal with in his time as ambassador, first of which was facing the European anger over the Finnish war the Soviet Union was prosecuting. More difficult to justify and negotiate was the Soviet non-aggression pact with Germany and the subsequent invasion of Poland. The Soviet Union and Nazi Germany entered into an infamous, if uneasy, pact that was to divide Poland between them. Hitler's forces invaded Poland in the early hours of 1 September 1939, beginning their brutal drive across the country. However, the most surprising part was yet to come when, on 17 September, the Soviet Union entered Polish territory, sealing Poland's fate, as it would turn out, for the next fifty years.

Stalin had acted on the secret clauses contained within the German–Soviet non-aggression pact signed only a month before that effectively split Poland between the two nations. Claiming their non-aggression pact with Poland was no longer valid as the Polish government had left Warsaw, with the timing calculated to ensure that Allied forces did not declare war on the Soviet Union, the Soviet Army swept across Poland to claim their share of the spoils.

Come June 1941, there was to be drastic change in the military and political situation when the Nazis surprised the Russians with Operation Barbarossa: the German invasion of the Soviet Union.

Maisky was first charged with normalising relationships with Great Britain and the other Allied nations. Churchill offered unconditional assistance before it was asked for, but the Polish camp was understandably more reluctant. Maisky, being based in London, was well placed to deal with the Polish government in exile and, as such, set about negotiating terms. Anthony Eden was pressurising Sikorski to come to terms with Stalin while simultaneously ensuring that he did not offend them in any way. It is probably fair to say that Sikorski was a realist when it came to this debate, knowing that he had to come to terms with the Soviets or else he would find himself, and Poland, marginalised in what had become a much wider conflict. Eden kept pushing for an agreement and eventually one was reached, allowing the two sides to work towards a solution based on Maisky's four points:

1. The treaties of 1939 between the Soviet Union and Germany to be made void
2. Diplomatic relations to be restored
3. Both governments to declare readiness to fight Germany
4. A Polish Army to be formed in Russia

The talks were protracted, especially concerning the Polish eastern frontier and the fate of Polish POWs, but the pressure was mounting on Sikorski. Eventually, after the news that Sir Stafford Cripps, the British ambassador to the Soviet Union, had secured an amnesty for all Polish citizens and that there was to be a British note in the treaty stating they would not recognise any changes to the Polish borders since 1939, Sikorski signed on 30 July 1941.

Maisky was recalled to Russia in 1943 and replaced by Gusev, who saw out the remainder of the war. Before he left, Maisky was also responsible for one other act: the removal of the railings surrounding the building with a blowtorch for donation to the British war effort.

No. 13 Kensington Palace Gardens is still the official residence of the Russian ambassador to this day. In 1991 the rent period was extended for ninety-nine years, with the Russian ambassador paying a symbolic £1 a year in rent.

The London Cage, MI9 Interrogation Centre
6, 7 & 8 KENSINGTON PALACE GARDENS

Tube: Kensington High Street
Barclays Cycle Hire: Kensington Church Street, Kensington

KENSINGTON PALACE GARDENS can be found off Kensington Road, with numbers 6 to 8 being about halfway up on the left-hand side as you head up the Kensington Road end, just before the Norwegian ambassador's London residence.

It being one of the most exclusive streets in London back in the 1940s, much as it is now, it is perhaps surprising to learn that from 1940 to 1948 some most unpleasant things were occurring behind the doors of 6, 7 & 8 Kensington Palace Gardens.

The three buildings became the Combined Services Detailed Interrogation Centre (CSDIC), more commonly known as 'the London Cage', and were under the control of MI9. Originally MI9a, it was responsible for 'enemy prisoners', but was still controlled by Crockatt and MI9 (see p. 129 on MI9).

Run by Lieutenant Colonel Alexander Scotland, who had been brought out of retirement, the centre was used to interrogate prisoners, either to discover information of interest or to extract confessions. In principle, this was not a problem and it was standard practice to interrogate prisoners to get vital information, but the methods used have been accused of being more analogous to those of the Gestapo than the British Army.

Run between 1940 and 1948, over 3,500 people are thought to have passed through the CSDIC, with many telling of routine mistreatment. Sleep deprivation, reduced rations and casual beatings were common, but more extreme 'treatments' were also dealt out. These included such torments as being made to walk in a tight circle for hours on end, continuous and extreme physical exercise and regular dousing with ice-cold water. All this was accompanied by regular beatings and humiliations. The International Red Cross apparently, by accident, discovered the presence of the CSDIC, but were denied entry for eighteen months, by which time the centre was closing down.

Scotland was proud of his work at CSDIC and appears to have felt he did nothing wrong. His book eventually went on sale in the late 1950s after a seven-year delay while the government tried to prevent its publication, and then ensured the book was heavily censored. However, it did back up the allegations of prisoners who were unlucky enough to enter the Cage. How widely the methods used in the Cage were known is unclear, but Scotland was certainly charged with no offence.

These three houses are now some of the most expensive private properties in London and have multimillion-pound price tags.

Secret Intelligence Service, Norwegian Training School
14 BROMPTON SQUARE

Tube: Knightsbridge
Barclays Cycle Hire: Holy Trinity Brompton, Knightsbridge

BROMPTON SQUARE can be found off the Brompton Road and is only a few roads up from the Natural History and Victoria & Albert museums.

At the early stages of the war, an immediate return to Norway by conventional forces was unlikely, so working for SIS gave Norwegian citizens the opportunity to immediately re-join the fight against the Nazis. SIS had no problem in acquiring Norwegians who were willing to work for them, with a continuing supply of new recruits arriving from their homeland.

The head of the Norwegian Section, P.9, set up a training school at the small house in Brompton Square. Here, prospective agents were taught the necessary field craft that would allow them to carry out operations for SIS in occupied Norway. This could include anything from armed or unarmed combat, first aid and photography to communication techniques, security and how to use dead letter boxes. At the end of training the agents were inserted into Norway by any means possible – given the country's long coastline, this often meant by submarine or boat.

By June 1943, there were twenty-two SIS networks operating in Norway gathering information on the enemy. Shore stations were responsible for collecting information on German naval movements, with special interest being paid to the location of *Tirpitz*. *Tirpitz* was assigned to Norway with the aim of engaging the northern convoys heading around Scandinavia to Russia. A constant problem for Allied shipping, *Tirpitz* was not put out of action until November 1944, although SIS intelligence had been used to launch an unsuccessful midget submarine raid on the ship in 1943.

SIS operatives would collect information from agents and by direct observation. One agent, Olsen, on his second six-month spell in Norway, was based in a camp with his colleagues overlooking the fjord entrance to Kristiansand. From here they were able to report on the German military units in

No. 14 Brompton Square, used by SIS during the war, as it is today.

the area, sometimes up to ten times a day – intelligence that was vital to the war effort.

No. 14 Brompton Square is, like most of the houses in the square, in residential occupation.

Secret Intelligence Service, Communications Section VIII
HANS PLACE

Tube: Knightsbridge
Barclays Cycle Hire: Pont Street, Knightsbridge

HANS PLACE is a London garden square that can be found just behind Harrods department store in Knightsbridge.

Communications Section VIII was set up by a man called Richard Gambier-Perry. Technically gifted, Gambier-Perry was described as the 'voice of Ultra' and was responsible for securely transmitting information decrypted by the Goverment Code and Cypher School (GC&CS) at Bletchley Park to ministries, governments in exile and commanders in the field.

In 1941, Section VIII took over the Radio Security Service that was managed by the General Post Office under War Office and MI5 supervision.

Much of the work carried out by Section VIII was at Whaddon Hall, after moving out of Bletchley Park itself (the large area was considered too much of a giveaway about what was happening there). Whaddon Hall was to get a military cover name, the 'Special Communication Unit', to account for the increased activity there. Much of the decrypted traffic from Bletchley Park went to Whaddon Hall, where it was transmitted onwards. Section VIII was responsible for all forms of secret communication and Gambier-Perry was credited with its modernisation. One of the great advances was with signals liaison units. These could be either fixed in buildings or mobile units, with associated equipment and staff, which would accompany field commanders. Many of the mobile signals liaison units were to work alongside the Allied units advancing across Europe after D-Day.

As such, Section VIII was responsible for constructing and equipping all these units, as well as training operators in the use of the equipment. Much of this training was carried out at the SIS training school at Hans Place, which was responsible for training over 600 operators.

Hans Place is made up mainly of older residential buildings, but there are some newer buildings on the western side built on the site of the original bomb-damaged buildings.

Special Operations Executive Camouflage Section, XVa

56 QUEEN'S GATE

Tube: Gloucester Road
Barclays Cycle Hire: Natural History Museum, South Kensington

QUEEN'S GATE runs from Hyde Park down to the Old Brompton Road and passes the Natural History Museum, opposite which No. 56, an old six-storey building, can be found.

The fledgling SOE soon found it had many problems to deal with and departments mushroomed up, and rapidly expanded, to fulfil operational requirements. One of these departments was the Camouflage Section, XV. Section XV initially took over the Queen's Gate building and one of the Victoria & Albert Museum's workshops in February 1942 and by June had moved into the Thatched Barn building near Elstree film studios. The Queen's Gate workshop was retained and given the designation XVa.

The Camouflage Section was responsible for concealing objects in everyday items, such as film, wireless sets and other paraphernalia that SOE agents were required to carry, but had to be hidden from an inquisitive enemy. They were also responsible for making weapons of sabotage look like common objects, such as explosives that looked like coal or dead rats.

SOE's Camouflage Section's first address, 56 Queen's Gate, as it looks today.

The section was headed by the larger-than-life character of Captain J. Elder Wills. After being declined entry to the air force and navy on the grounds that he weighed in at 18 stone, had a leg injury and was deaf in one ear, he joined the Army as a camouflage officer. After returning to England wounded, he continued his work making dummy vehicles to fool Luftwaffe reconnaissance flights over Britain. In January 1942 he set up SOE's Camouflage Section, which quickly expanded into the Queen's Gate building. Recruiting people from the film and theatre industry, in which he had worked before the war, he soon had possibly one of the most eclectic teams of any government department.

Wills set about acquiring all manner of materials that would be useful to Section XV's work, including a Belgian gas meter, 150 rat skins and 100 varieties of coal. With all these stores, Wills and his technicians at Queen's Gate were soon producing a vast array of ingenious devices. It would seem that nothing was beyond this team, whose work included shoes containing plastic explosive and a time-delay fuse, lipstick holders capable of concealing messages, an exploding tobacco box and a grenade disguised as a tube of toothpaste.

The available space at Queen's Gate was soon outstripped by demand for more and more items from Wills's team. The majority of the section moved up to the Thatched Barn building, but Queen's Gate was retained, where research was carried out on prototypes and agents going into or returning from operations were briefed.

The nineteenth-century building at 56 Queen's Gate has since been divided into separate flats for residential use.

Special Operations Executive Photographic and Make-Up Section, XVc
2 & 3 TREVOR SQUARE

Tube: Knightsbridge
Barclays Cycle Hire: Montpelier Street, Knightsbridge

TREVOR SQUARE is linked by Trevor Street to Knightsbridge and Hyde Park to the north and links to the Old Brompton Road to the south, coming out directly opposite Harrods. To the southern end of Trevor Square is a building that was used by Harrods as a depot and for the production of own-brand goods until the 1970s.

SOE's Camouflage Section expanded into other niche areas of work as more problems were encountered that required specialist expertise. The Photographic

Nos 2 & 3 in the corner of Trevor Square were used by SOE's Photographic Section.

and Make-Up Section, designated XVc, took up residence at 2 & 3 Trevor Square in March 1943.

The people working for the Make-Up Section were recruited mainly from the film industry to develop ways in which agents could alter their appearance when on operations. This led to another problem, as an agent who had altered their appearance would naturally require identity papers showing them in that disguise. The Photographic Section was responsible for assembling all the images of an agent required for their forged identity papers. This was an enormous task and by the end of the war 1,620 agents had been photographed, along with nearly 2,000 men and women for military passes and producing enlargements for the Records Section.

The buildings at 2 & 3 Trevor Square are now privately owned and are in residential use.

Special Operations Executive Demonstration Room
NATURAL HISTORY MUSEUM, CROMWELL ROAD

Tube: South Kensington
Barclays Cycle Hire: Natural History Museum, South Kensington

The Natural History Museum in London has been enlightening the population to nature's secrets since 1753, when a private collection became part of the

The Natural History Museum: home to dinosaurs and the SOE demonstration room.

British Museum, and can be found next to the Victoria & Albert Museum on CROMWELL ROAD in Kensington.

The Natural History Museum became the home of an SOE demonstration room that came under the auspice of Camouflage Section as Section XVb. The ground-floor room that was to become the demonstration room allowed other SOE departments to view the equipment being produced, thus ensuring they were up to date with the most current devices available for operations. Generally only senior SOE officials and some agents were given access to the room, but the king and his family are known to have been regular visitors. The equipment being produced was innovative, novel and gave scientists and engineers the opportunity to test their ingenuity to the limit.

The demonstration room has long since been retired, but the Natural History Museum remains one of London's most popular attractions.

The area of London known as Belgravia is enclosed by Sloane Street to the west, Grosvenor Place, near Buckingham Palace, to the east and Hyde Park in the north.

The area is home to a plethora of embassies, many of which can be found in Belgrave Square, such as the old Embassy of Yugoslavia (now the Embassy of Serbia and Montenegro), the Norwegian Embassy and the Belgian Embassy. Many other embassy buildings can be found on the surrounding streets, such as Luxembourg's, which is on Wilton Crescent.

The area was also home, at different times before and after the war, to some of the war's most notable figures. Lord Gort, commander-in-chief of the BEF, lived at 33 Belgrave Square from 1920 to 1926. Lord Mountbatten lived at Chester Street during the war and then moved just off the square at 2 Wilton Crescent until his death in 1979. Neville Chamberlain lived south of Belgrave Square at 37 Eaton Square from 1923 to 1935. All of these buildings, apart from Mountbatten's wartime residence, are marked by prominent blue plaques.

One of the most famous residents of Belgravia during the war was Ian Fleming, creator of James Bond, who lived on Ebury Street, which is a stone's throw from the grounds of Buckingham Palace.

The main centre of Belgravia, around Belgrave Square and towards Eton Gardens, is worth a visit as it is one of the most tranquil parts of London, possibly because of the absence of any shops or pubs. With so many embassies in such a compact area, it can only be imagined what political dealings have occurred between them and Britain throughout the years.

KEY

1. Hyde Park
2. Luxembourg Embassy
3. Lord Mountbatten's Wartime Residence
4. Yugoslavian Embassy
5. Belgian Volunteers
6. Ian Fleming's Wartime Residence

Hyde Park
KNIGHTSBRIDGE

Tube: Queensway, Lancaster Gate, Marble Arch, Hyde Park Corner, Knightsbridge
Barclays Cycle Hire: several throughout the park

The park was originally acquired by Henry VIII in 1536 as a royal hunting ground. It was not until 100 years later in 1637, when James I came to the throne, that the park was opened to the general public. Hyde Park now covers a vast expanse of London; its north-east corner can be found at the western (Marble Arch) end of Oxford Street and is bordered by the Bayswater Road to the north, Kensington Road to the south and Park Lane to the east.

Hyde Park was the scene of frantic activity once Prime Minister Neville Chamberlain had declared war. Once the initial air-raid sirens had proven to be false, works started in the park excavating earth for use in sandbags to protect the many important buildings around London. It was also used by the Auxiliary Fire Service for training purposes during the war.

Later on in the war, during the Blitz, the park was to be home to a heavy anti-aircraft battery defending the capital from the nightly Luftwaffe raids. It was near these guns that a police war reserve constable was fatally stabbed after he approached a man who had been seen 'lying on his stomach facing towards the guns apparently writing something on a piece of paper' and then at 'short intervals he looked up at the guns and then continued writing', according to the Metropolitan Police. Frank Cobbett, a labourer of no fixed abode, was sentenced to death for murder, but this was reduced on appeal to manslaughter and fifteen years' imprisonment.

The park was to be bombed several times, with one huge 1,800kg 'Satan' bomb fortuitously landing in the Serpentine rather than the surrounding residential areas.

Hyde Park is a wonderful open space that can be visited away from the busier aspects of the capital, while it is also a venue for concerts and shows.

One of the many Barclay's Cycle Hire racks to be found in Hyde Park.

Luxembourg Embassy
27 WILTON CRESCENT

Tube: Hyde Park Corner
Barclays Cycle Hire: Grosvenor Crescent, Belgravia

The Embassy of Luxembourg can still be found at 27 WILTON CRESCENT, which is just off Belgrave Square.

The Grand Duchy of Luxembourg, bordering Belgium, Germany and France, was never in much of a position to influence the events of the Second World War. While its government's sympathies clearly did not lie with the Nazis, there was little they could do but reiterate their neutral status. This neutrality,

along with several other countries', was violated on 10 May when the 1st Panzer Division, accompanied by Heinz Guderian, entered the country.

The Grand Duchess of Luxembourg resided in London with her government in exile, led by Pierre Dupong, and would have relied on her embassy and its staff at Wilton Crescent for the day-to-day running of their affairs until they could return to Luxembourg in 1944.

The Luxembourg Embassy, still found on Wilton Crescent.

Lord Mountbatten's Wartime Residence
15 CHESTER STREET

Tube: Hyde Park Corner
Barclays Cycle Hire: Belgrave Square, Belgravia

No. 15 CHESTER STREET became Lord Louis Mountbatten and his wife's London home for most of the war, while their Broadlands estate in Hampshire was turned into a hospital for injured servicemen. Chester Street can be found directly off Grosvenor Place, a road which runs alongside the gardens of Buckingham Palace.

Lord Louis Mountbatten, great grandson to Queen Victoria and a much-loved member of the royal family, was also highly ambitious and used, in part, his influence at the highest levels of society to progress his naval career.

Mountbatten, throughout the Second World War, gradually rose to fill one of the highest positions of command. Starting out on HMS *Kelly*, flagship of the 5th Destroyer Flotilla, he saw action in Norway and on anti-submarine patrols. After several near misses he was to lose *Kelly* in the Battle of Crete, where, watching from the bridge, Mountbatten saw a Stuka dive-bomber release its bomb which he was able to follow down until it impacted on a gun deck. *Kelly* eventually rolled over and sank; its survivors were machine-gunned in the water by the German planes.

From this role he moved on to become the Chief of Combined Operations in 1942, a role that was responsible for developing tactics for amphibious assault. The Combined Operations Command reflected the need for elements of all three services to co-ordinate their methods to ensure success. The spearhead of this unit was the commandos, whose first mission was the gallant yet futile attack on Dieppe. Mountbatten, as head of Combined Ops, shouldered much of the blame for the raid, described by Ian Fleming as a 'bloody gallant affair'. The raid had changed in format from its original conception of a pincer attack to a full frontal attack without any kind of preceding bombardment, and delayed twice before it went ahead to its bloody conclusion.

From Combined Ops and Dieppe, Mountbatten went on to one of the highest commands in the Allied structure when he was appointed as the Supreme Allied Commander of South East Asia by Churchill. With the

Lord Louis Mountbatten's home during the war after he moved out of his Broadlands estate, which was in use as a hospital.

Supreme Commander for the cross-Channel invasion being an American, it was agreed that the reciprocal position in Asia would be taken by someone form the British forces. Many names came and went, either vetoed by the Americans or Churchill, until they eventually agreed on Mountbatten, who took up the position in November 1943. In this command he had the unenviable task of having to deal with competing personalities from the American, British and Chinese armies. Mountbatten was to lead the South East Asia Command through the war to eventual victory over the Japanese in Burma – something that is of enormous credit to him. One of his final acts of the war was to receive the formal surrender of the Japanese forces in Singapore on 5 September 1945.

Mountbatten went on to become the last viceroy and first governor general of India, and finally the First Sea Lord. Lord Mountbatten was killed by a terrorist bomb hidden aboard his boat in 1979 at his holiday home in Mullaghmore, County Sligo. Two teenage boys and the Dowager Lady Brabourne were also killed in the attack.

Yugoslavian Embassy
28 BELGRAVE SQUARE

Tube: Hyde Park Corner
Barclays Cycle Hire: Belgrave Square, Belgravia

The building that was the Yugoslavian Embassy can be found on the south side of BELGRAVE SQUARE, which is a short walk from Buckingham Palace, at No. 28.

Hitler had been expanding his Reich across Europe, taking over countries by threat or direct action with impunity. Come April 1941 his attentions turned to Greece and Yugoslavia. Prior to the invasion of Russia it was deemed necessary to 'clear the southern flank' and a directive was issued, Operation Marita, which, as its primary objective, was to occupy the northern coast of the Adriatic. Yugoslavia posed little direct threat to Hitler, but was strategically important, effectively blocking the way to Greece. Hitler simply issued terms to the Yugoslavian government that would effectively turn the country into another satellite state, assuming that the people would not be so foolish as to refuse. King Paul, faced by the most efficient military machine in the world, accepted as anticipated. However, the Yugoslavian people did not. King Paul was deposed, Prince Peter put on the throne and Hitler, in his wrath, ordered his forces to invade. This was Operation Punishment: a pitiless campaign that started on 6 April 1941 and saw tens of thousands of people killed, Belgrade destroyed and the country overrun with in a few days.

King Peter fled to Britain and exile in May 1941, where King George VI assumed responsibility for him. It was upon his arrival in Britain that he met and fell in love with Princess Alexandra of Greece, another royal exile. In 1944 King George gave his formal permission for them to be wed in London. The king served as King Peter's best man at the ceremony held at the Yugoslavian Embassy on 20 March, which was attended by much of the deposed royalty residing in London at the time.

King Peter and his new wife were never to return to Yugoslavia to regain his throne as the monarchy was dissolved in 1945 and the country became a communist state for the next four decades. King Peter died at the age of 47 and his son, Crown Prince Alexander has returned to Serbia where he is campaigning for the reintroduction of a constitutional monarchy. The embassy is still in use today, but is now the Embassy of Serbia and Montenegro.

Belgian Volunteers
103 BELGRAVE PLACE

Tube: Hyde Park Corner
Barclays Cycle Hire: Eaton Square, Belgravia

BELGRAVE PLACE is a street running off Belgrave Square, with No. 103 being about halfway down and marked by a metal plaque.

Belgium, hoping to remain out of the looming conflict, had declared neutrality. To respect this neutrality, the Belgian government refused to allow British and French forces to position themselves on their territory for fear that Hitler would use this 'provocative act' as an excuse to invade. Their efforts were to be in vain as, to advance on France, the Germans planned to go through Belgium to avoid the Maginot Line, and on 10 May 1940 the German Army crossed the Belgian border.

As soon as the German advance had been reported, the British and French forces moved up to occupy positions around the River Dyle, but they were soon forced into all out retreat. The Belgian Army, unable to hold back the invaders, was caught up in the rout and on 27 May, feeling they could do no more, King Leopold capitulated and ordered his troops to lay down their arms the following day.

While Leopold remained in Belgium, the Belgian Cabinet moved to France and then England, where they formed a government in exile. Many Belgians rallied to the cause and it was at this building at 103 Belgrave Place that many volunteered to carry on the fight to liberate their country.

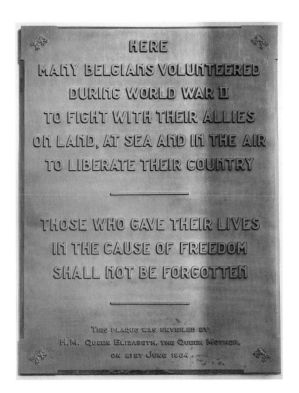

HERE
MANY BELGIANS VOLUNTEERED
DURING WORLD WAR II
TO FIGHT WITH THEIR ALLIES
ON LAND, AT SEA AND IN THE AIR
TO LIBERATE THEIR COUNTRY

THOSE WHO GAVE THEIR LIVES
IN THE CAUSE OF FREEDOM
SHALL NOT BE FORGOTTEN

THIS PLAQUE WAS UNVEILED BY
H.M. QUEEN ELIZABETH, THE QUEEN MOTHER,
ON 21ST JUNE 1964

The plaque found on 103 Belgrave Place commemorating those Belgians who volunteered to fight for the Allied cause.

Ian Fleming's Wartime Residence
22A EBURY STREET

Tube: Victoria
Barclays Cycle Hire: Eton Square, Belgravia

22A EBURY STREET can be found only a short distance from the back of Buckingham Palace and Victoria station and was the home of Ian Fleming, known worldwide as creator of the James Bond books and the multimillion-pound film franchise that they have spawned.

Fleming's wartime work could have come out of the pages of one of his Bond books and many aspects of those books were drawn from his wartime experiences. However, there was nothing fictional about the work he, and his colleagues, carried out during the war.

The Naval Intelligence Department (NID) origins date back to the 1880s, when it was tasked with finding out information on other nations' naval forces. In January 1939 a new Director of Naval Intelligence (DNI) was appointed, Admiral John Godfrey, the real-life model for Fleming's fictional MI6 head 'M'. Godfrey, though not from an intelligence background, set about improving the organisation and moving it to a war footing. In this task he was greatly helped by the former DNI Admiral Sir Reggie Hall, who was to advise Godfrey that aside from his personal secretary, a civilian role, he would benefit from a uniformed 'fixer' and the word was put out. It was the Governor of the Bank of England who recommended Fleming, and at a lunch meeting in the Grill Room of the Carlton Hotel he met Godfrey. From this meeting Fleming was to join NID for a stint that would last six years.

NID was one of the most intriguing groups to be found within the Admiralty, made ever more so by their activities throughout the war. Fleming was to work in Room 39, which overlooked Horse Guards Parade, while Room 38 was Godfrey's office and Room 19 held the NID telephone switchboard with its direct lines to the prime minister, Foreign Office and intelligence directorates.

From Room 39, Fleming was to set in motion many innovative plans, but none were more daring or imaginative as the creation of 30 Assault Unit, a group of commandos tasked with 'pinching' enemy material, as Fleming put it.

The need to acquire enemy material of importance had much to do with the work being carried out by the men and women at Bletchley Park. In their quest to unravel the Enigma codes they were constantly pressing for more source material. Some useful code books and machine parts were acquired from the Narvik affair in Norway, but Fleming clearly appreciated the need

The wartime home of Ian Fleming, creator of secret agent 007, on Ebury Street, is marked with a plaque.

for more proactive measures, with one suggestion being to ditch a captured German plane in the Channel and capture the German rescue vessel.

The fledgling idea took off in July 1942 with a pair of meetings involving Fleming and members of SIS, MI5 and Combined Operations Intelligence. It was agreed that a platoon of handpicked Royal Marine Commandos would form Fleming's Intelligence Assault Unit (IAU).

Their first mission was set to run as part of the famous Dieppe raid. In terms of casualties, the raid was a disaster, but it provided many lessons that would be implemented in future landings, including the North African and D-Day landings. The inaugural IAU mission also failed in its objective to steal German navy cipher machines, code books and secret documents from their Dieppe headquarters after their gunboat sustained a direct hit.

Undeterred, the development of the IAU continued and come November 1942 they were back in action, with much greater success. Accompanying the Anglo–US invasion of Vichy French-occupied North Africa, they were heading to Algiers. Eventually landing and finding their target, they were able to justify their existence when they discovered an Abwehr variant Enigma machine which, along with 2 tons of documents, was taken back to Britain.

In the preparations for the cross-Channel invasion, Fleming set about the reorganisation and expansion of IAU to 30 Assault Unit (30 AU) and the development of a corresponding division, located in the Admiralty Citadel (NID 30). No. 30 AU were tasked with entering occupied Europe with the vanguard forces to capture any information that could be of use both in ensuring the ultimate victory and in a post-war world. The unit was to have some stunning success, such as the capture of all German naval records from 1870 to the present date in Schloss Tambach, near Coburg. In another daring move, 30 AU raced into Kiel ahead of the Russians, crossing the Second Army's armistice halt line. In Kiel they captured Dr Hellmuth Walter and the factory bearing his name, where much work was being undertaken in submarine propulsion using hydrogen peroxide. This propulsion system was to be used in the V1 and V2 programmes, torpedoes and the Messerschmitt Me 163, a prototype jet plane.

In 1946, 30 AU were disbanded and Ian Fleming went on to international fame with his secret agent, 007, whose many exploits have their genesis in Fleming's own wartime history and that of the unit he created and ran from the Admiralty.

The district of Marylebone stretches from the west corner of Regent's Park and carries on south to Oxford Street, going as far east as Portland Street.

Marylebone suffered from German bombing during the war, although not as extensively as many other areas of London. Madame Tussauds was hit in 1940, destroying its cinema (which was replaced by the Planetarium) and 352 wax head moulds. It was fortunate that these bombs did not land a little further west as the area around Baker Street had become the command centre for Britain's clandestine operations in Europe.

The newly formed Special Operations Executive (SOE) set up its headquarters at 64 Baker Street and rapidly expanded into other buildings nearby. There are probably few more inconspicuous buildings in London that have been home to such a captivating part of history as those in Marylebone.

A monument to the men and women who served with SOE can be found on the Embankment, close to Lambeth Palace (see SOE Memorial, p. 205).

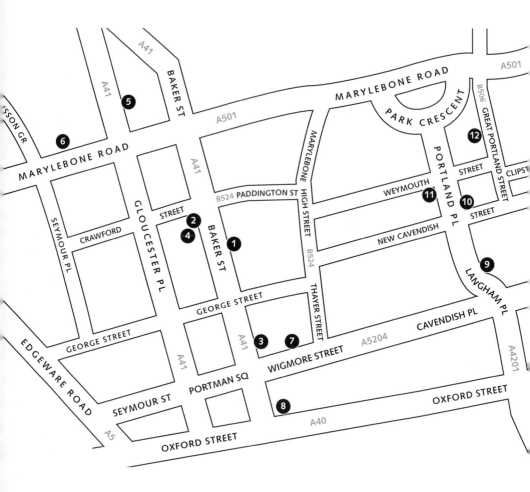

KEY

1. SOE Headquarters
2. SOE Offices, Norgeby House
3. SOE Flat
4. SOE Signals Directorate
5. SOE, RF Section
6. Grand Central Hotel
7. Free French Counter-Espionage Unit
8. Selfridges Department Store
9. BBC Broadcasting House
10. Military Intelligence Research Unit, Development Laboratory
11. Polish Government in Exile and Sikorski Statue
12. Ed Murrow's Wartime Residence

Special Operations Executive Headquarters

64 BAKER STREET

Tube: Baker Street
Barclays Cycle Hire: Baker Street

BAKER STREET runs from north to south across the Marylebone Road, with No. 64 being located halfway down on the southern side. No. 64 Baker Street is now used as shops and offices and is marked by a green plaque.

The Special Operations Executive was set up in the aftermath of the Dunkirk evacuation when it was quickly realised that Britain would have a very limited ability to strike back at Nazi Germany by conventional means.

The most famous line often quoted is Churchill's demand to Hugh Dalton to 'set Europe ablaze', and this is exactly what SOE set out to do. SOE was not created from scratch, but was an amalgamation of several other departments from three other organisations: D Section (also known as Section IX) of the Secret Intelligence Service (SIS), the Military Intelligence Research Unit (MI(R) of the War Office) and Electra House, which was attached to the Foreign Office, mainly producing and countering propaganda.

After some wrangling about its exact charter, SOE's creation was formally approved by the War Cabinet on 22 July 1940, principally to train agents to act as saboteurs and encourage local resistance movements in occupied countries. Churchill had already offered the ministerial responsibility of SOE to Hugh Dalton (although he was to be replaced by Lord Selborne in 1942); hence SOE nominally came under the umbrella of his charge, the Ministry of Economic Warfare.

In October 1940, SOE moved from its offices at Caxton Street (where D Section had been) into the much larger building at 64 Baker Street, which had just been vacated by the Prison Commissioners. Since even the name of SOE was a closely guarded secret that was not revealed until after the war, it was given the civilian cover name of the 'Inter Services Research Bureau', which adorned the Baker Street offices.

The director of SOE was known as 'CD', the first being Sir Frank Nelson, whose office was at 64 Baker Street. When Lord Selborne took over ministerial control of SOE, Nelson was replaced by Sir Charles Hambro. Major General Colin Gubbins was the final and probably most influential director of SOE, taking over from Hambro in August 1943.

To achieve its overall aims of 'promoting sabotage and subversion through its own covert agents and with supplying arms, equipment and agents to resistance movements throughout occupied Europe and beyond' (*SOE the Scientific Secrets*, Boyce and Everett, 2004), SOE began a rapid expansion reaching a peak of around 13,000 staff. To deal with ever swelling ranks, the nature and structure of SOE continually evolved. Departments expanded and then were divided, with smaller groups being swept up and repositioned along the way. However, the basic structure that resulted divided the organisation into two main categories, 'Operations' and 'Research and Development'.

Operations was responsible for any mission into enemy territory and sent agents behind the lines to gather intelligence, commit acts of sabotage or assist local resistance movements. Each country had its own department, varying in size depending on the scale of operations being carried out in its sphere of influence.

Research and Development was overseen by Professor Dudley Newitt and created equipment to aid SOE missions into enemy-occupied territories. SOE's Research and Development group devised a whole host of innovative gadgets and weapons, from the Welrod – a single-shot silenced pistol – and radios hidden in biscuit tins to miniature submarines.

After the war, as SOE was disbanded, many staff simply returned to their pre-war occupations, although a small number were incorporated into SIS.

Special Operations Executive Offices, Norgeby House
83 BAKER STREET

Tube: Baker Street
Barclays Cycle Hire: Baker Street

Norgeby House can be found at 83 BAKER STREET, a few hundred metres up and on the opposite side of the road to SOE's main offices at 64 Baker Street. Currently the building is used as shops and offices.

SOE's expansion was rapid and it soon took over Norgeby House at 83 Baker Street. The offices at Norgeby House also expanded into the top two floors of the adjacent building at No. 82, Michael House, the corporate headquarters of the shopping chain Marks & Spencer. As their offices expanded around the Baker Street area, SOE soon started calling themselves the Baker Street Irregulars.

Norgeby House primarily housed the 'country sections'. Each country of operations had its own section, such as Belgium, Denmark, Yugoslavia, Czechoslovakia, Holland or Norway, though the biggest section of all covered France. Each section was simply prefixed with its country of operations, so there was the French Section, Belgian Section, Dutch Section and so on.

Each of the country sections had its own problems to contend with. The Dutch Section suffered some serious reverses when its networks were penetrated by the Germans. It was some time before it was realised, and

The well-marked 83 Baker Street was home to many of SOE's 'country sections'.

accepted, that many of the agents being dropped into Holland were falling straight into the hands of the Gestapo.

The Danish Section had a bigger problem in persuading higher authorities that a country the size of Denmark could have much to offer in terms of intelligence. The first agents were dropped into Denmark blind – that is, they did not have any contacts in the country to rely on. Of the first two agents sent in, one died when his parachute failed to open. The other, Mogens Hammer, enjoyed great success preparing the ground for further agents, even preaching to German troops in his disguise as a Protestant parson.

The Norwegian Section carried out one of the most famous SOE sabotage raids of the war. Code-named Operation Grouse (with Operation Gunnerside being put into effect to support it), this was the mission that was to destroy the chemical plant at Vermok, where the Germans were producing heavy water, a prerequisite for early atomic weapons. In this famous raid, nine Norwegians managed to infiltrate the plant, destroy it and make good their escape.

Special Operations Executive Flat
ORCHARD COURT, PORTMAN SQUARE

Tube: Baker Street
Barclays Cycle Hire: Baker Street

ORCHARD COURT can be found off Portman Square, which is at the southern end of Baker Street and is a short walk from SOE's Baker Street HQ. Currently the building is made up of private apartments and offices.

The French Section of SOE, or simply F Section, used a flat in Orchard Court to meet new recruits and to brief agents before sending them out on field operations. It was a four-bedroom flat on the second floor of Orchard Court, sparsely furnished and rarely big enough; new recruits were made to wait in the bathroom, with its jet-black tub and onyx bidet.

Orchard Court was used rather than the Baker Street HQ as a security precaution to ensure that potential recruits did not see any classified material. It also ensured agents heading into Europe would have as little information about their parent organisation as possible in case they were captured by the Gestapo and interrogated.

The man in charge of F Section from 1941 was Maurice Buckmaster, a veteran of the Dunkirk retreat. He had been working as a manager at the Ford

The entrance to Orchard Court, through which many an agent destined for Europe must have passed to be briefed before heading out on their missions.

Motor Company in France prior to the war, then served in the Intelligence Corps before returning to England. Buckmaster himself would often interview prospective agents in Orchard Court before passing off the successful candidates to his assistant, Vera Atkins.

Agents waiting at Orchard Court before departing into Europe were, as far as possible, able to relax there. One F Section member of staff, Elizabeth Norman, responsible for SOE agents, recalled 'feeding éclairs to Odette as we waited for the moon to come up in the right place'. Odette was eventually captured and ended up at Ravensbrück concentration camp at the same time as Violette Szabo. However, while Szabo was to be executed, Odette would return in the most extraordinary circumstances. The Ravensbrück Kommandant Fritz Suhren took her from her cell and drove her to the advancing Americans in the hope that Odette would save him at any future trial. She did not and Suhren was officially sentenced for his war crimes in 1950.

Special Operations Executive Signals Directorate
MONTAGU MANSIONS

Tube: Baker Street
Barclays Cycle Hire: Baker Street

MONTAGU MANSIONS is an apartment block on a road of the same name which links Crawford Street and Dorset Street, both of which are just off Baker Street. The apartments used by SOE returned to private ownership directly after the war.

By the end of 1943, SOE's continual expansion meant that another move was required and the Signals Directorate left Norgeby House and took up residence in Montagu Mansions.

The Signals Directorate itself was under the control of Colonel F.W. Nicholls and was responsible for all communication with agents in the occupied countries, and therefore responsible for the codes used by them.

At the onset of the war, agents' messages were encoded using the 'poem code', its frailties either not realised or ignored. A basic code needs a method to convert the message being transmitted into a code. In the early days of SOE, this was done by using a poem or famous quotation as the code key. Something easily memorable was used for security reasons, the idea being that if an agent were caught the code key would not be written down and they would have no incriminating papers on them. Into this were added security checks, such as deliberate spelling mistakes that were used to let London know if the agent was acting under duress or not.

Montagu Mansions, where SOE's expanding Signals Directorate moved for the later part of the war.

The fragility of the poem code was revealed by Leo Marks – one of the more colourful characters to emerge from SOE – in that it was actually very easy for the enemy to break the code as the same code key was being used for every message. A further problem was that one mistake by the wireless operator in the field could mean that the message arriving at the London office was indecipherable and it would have to be re-sent.

Eventually, agents were sent into France with 'Worked Out Keys' printed on silk that were used once then burnt. Unlike using one poem to encode every message, a single unique code would be used each time.

The use of Worked Out Keys was one of many reasons why the Signals Directorate had expanded. Marks's plan meant that all the new code keys had to be constructed and printed on silk, which required significant resources. The new codes were a success and they were used until the end of the war. Subtle improvements were continually being made to improve security and lower the chance of indecipherable messages being received.

Special Operations Executive, RF Section

1 DORSET SQUARE

Tube: Baker Street
Barclays Cycle Hire: Dorset Square

No. 1 DORSET SQUARE, located east of Regent's Park, a few streets over from the northern end of Baker Street, can be found on the corner of Gloucester Place and Melcombe Street. Marked by a commemorative plaque, it housed the RF Section of SOE. It is currently in use as a French language school.

RF section was responsible for all Free French operations in occupied France, while F Section was a wholly British affair, and was one of many examples of the blurred operational lines within SOE. RF Section did report directly to SOE but was fiercely loyal to de Gaulle and the Free French. As a result, its staff were trusted by the Free French, but maintained some accountability to Baker Street. This was the closest any department came to bridging the gap between SOE and the Free French at Duke Street.

Many agents were sent out from Dorset Square to occupied France with varying degrees of success. One of the most remarkable figures who operated in RF section was 'Tommy' Yeo-Thomas, also known by the code name White Rabbit (see p. 134 on Yeo-Thomas's wartime residence in Guildford Street).

Grand Central Hotel

THE LANDMARK HOTEL, 222 MARYLEBONE ROAD

Tube: Marylebone
Barclays Cycle Hire: Harewood Avenue, Marylebone

The Grand Central Hotel, opened in 1899, was a magnificent and luxurious hotel that was located to serve visitors to London coming into Marylebone station. It can be found on the MARYLEBONE ROAD, just south of Marylebone station and west of Baker Street Underground station.

The problem of how to assist servicemen trying to return from enemy territory back to their own forces was taken on by Brigadier Norman Crockatt, the head of MI9, just before France was invaded. Over the course of the war MI9 developed training methods, escape lines and even organised large-scale operations, all with the aim of extracting Allied soldiers from occupied Europe.

Back in Britain, the newly returned men were often sent to the Grand Central Hotel in Marylebone, which had been requisitioned for military use. One of the departments resident there was MI9's interrogation centre for returned prisoners. It was here that Airey Neave was to find himself almost

The Landmark Hotel, previously known as the Grand Central Hotel. Its charm was somewhat lost when occupied by the military

two years after being captured by the Germans at Calais. Neave would go on to serve in MI9 with the cover name 'Saturday', with much of his experience being gained from his successful escape.

After being wounded in Calais, Neave found himself in Germany at Spangenburg POW camp and then Thorn in Poland. After a failed escape attempt from Thorn, Neave was moved to Colditz from where he successfully escaped. Dressed in German uniforms tailored from Dutch uniforms, he and others were able to walk past the sentries to get to the castle drawbridge. From there they went down into the dry moat and then up and over the outer wall, continuing by foot and train to the Swiss border.

Whilst recuperating in Switzerland, Neave was told to head home as MI9 had 'asked for him'. So began another journey across Vichy France and Spain to the Rock of Gibraltar and back to England and the MI9 interrogation at the Grand Central Hotel. A double bedroom converted to an office was used by the intelligence officer who questioned him and distilled the detail of his escapes 'to war office language' and ensured they were 'no more exciting than a report by the C.I.D. on their observation of a public convenience' (*Saturday at MI9*, Neave, 2010).

The Grand Central Hotel continued to be used by the military after the war before being acquired by the British Railway Board as offices. The building was returned to use as a hotel in the 1980s and is now called The Landmark London: one of the capital's most luxurious hotels.

Free French Counter-Espionage Unit
10 DUKE STREET

Tube: Baker Street
Barclays Cycle Hire: Baker Street

DUKE STREET can be found bisecting Oxford Street and Wigmore Street, with No. 10 being located on the north-western corner of those two streets. The building is now privately owned.

With Phillipe Pétain taking France to surrender and appeasement with Germany, the Free French, with Charles de Gaulle as their leader, began to arrive in Britain. He was determined, not only to rid France of its German occupiers, but to do so entirely on his own terms.

While de Gaulle's Free French HQ was in Carlton Terrace, near St James's Park, they also had a Free French Counter-Espionage Unit in Duke Street that had much the same mandate as SOE. However, as in many things, what could have been a mutually beneficial relationship turned into the complete opposite.

The man de Gaulle chose to be the head of Military Intelligence-Gathering and Operations was a teacher at the military training school at Saint-Cyr. His name was André Dewavrin, although he took on a pseudonym, 'Passy', after the Paris Metro station.

The French believed that they alone should run operations in France, with de Gaulle saying that by setting up their resistance networks in France the British 'were infringing French sovereignty'. Ultimately a special section of SOE, RF Section, was created specifically for dealing with Duke Street, although this did little to prevent the mutual distrust between the two sides.

Selfridges Department Store
400 OXFORD STREET

Tube: Bond Street
Barclays Cycle Hire: North Audley Street

Selfridges has, since 1909, been one of London's most fashionable stores and can be found towards the Marble Arch end of OXFORD STREET, close to Bond Street Underground station.

Selfridges, like most shops, continued to trade during the Second World War. However, shopping was not all that occurred at Selfridges. One of the basements of the store was converted to house US voice encryption technology developed by Bell Labs, called the X-System. Code-named

Selfridges, one of London's best-known department stores, was badly damaged by Luftwaffe raids.

SIGSALY, the system scrambled all communications and, by linking up to the War Rooms at Whitehall, allowed Churchill and Roosevelt to communicate via a secure telephone line.

Selfridges was to find itself firmly in the front line later in the war when it was hit by incendiary bombs. One of the heaviest raids of the war occurred on the night of 16–17 April. The damage across London was severe, and Selfridges was to be one of the many casualties.

Superintendent Fireman George Bennison, having been informed that there was a fifty-pump fire at Selfridges, arrived at the store to find its upper two floors well alight. With a lack of water hampering operations, an order was given to lay a special main from the Serpentine in Hyde Park to Marble Arch in order to service the fires raging up and down Oxford Street, but it was not until 9 a.m. on 17 April that the fires were finally brought under control. The bombing destroyed the famous roof gardens, which were never to reopen.

The US Army Signal Corps operating SIGSALY survived the April raid being deep in a sub-basement, although it was flooded after a nearby V1 flying bomb strike later in the war.

BBC Broadcasting House
PORTLAND PLACE

Tube: Oxford Circus
Barclays Cycle Hire: Broadcasting House

BBC Broadcasting House was built in 1932 and can be found at the southern end of PORTLAND PLACE where the road bends. It is still used by the BBC, with the building having undergone major renovations and extensions in 2011–12.

From the outset, it was clear that the BBC would play a vital role in any war, with radio being the principal method of communication with the British people and those in countries under occupation.

The problem facing Broadcasting House was the building itself. Made from white limestone, it was thought to present a conspicuous target for the Luftwaffe. Despite objections that it would not be possible to accurately target, the building was camouflaged, with its white exterior being transformed to a dull grey.

The newly refurbished BBC Broadcasting House, minus its war time camouflage and bomb damage.

Though this may or may not have prevented the deliberate targeting of Broadcasting House, it was still hit by German bombs. The first strike in December 1940 was the most devastating, with several BBC staff losing their lives. However, this did not stop newsreader Bruce Belfrage continuing with the nine o'clock broadcast. Belfrage was safely broadcasting from the depths of the building, and only a few fragments of plaster fell on him. Though the sound of the bomb detonating was heard by the millions of listeners, many did not realise what it was.

Broadcasting House was severely damaged again during the great raid of 16–17 April, when a parachute mine exploded outside the main entrance in Langham Place. Several members of staff were buried by the collapse of the gramophone records library, when 50 tons of records fell into their offices. All were released by rescuers with only minor injuries after a frustrating dig through the BBC's record archive.

An interesting aside for the BBC was their regular broadcasts of messages for people separated by the war. Many were, of course, genuine, but some were messages for SOE agents on the continent. Prearranged phrases known as 'action messages' were broadcast to alert resistance networks to the arrival of agents or arms drops. In occupied countries, just listening to these broadcasts could result in incarceration, as the Gestapo would enter houses and arrest those listening as suspected resistance members.

Military Intelligence Research Unit, Development Laboratory
36 PORTLAND PLACE

Tube: Oxford Circus
Barclays Cycle Hire: Portland Place

No. 36 PORTLAND PLACE can be found a few streets up from Broadcasting House on the eastern side of the street and was for sale at the time of writing.

At the outset of the war MI(R)c was a small operation which looked at the development of devices for guerrilla warfare. It was part of the Military Intelligence Research Unit (MI(R), previously known as GS(R), or General Staff Research). MI(R) was one of the three departments, along with D Section from MI6 and Electra House (which was responsible for propaganda), that were amalgamated to create the Special Operations Executive. However, despite its obvious overlap with D Section, MI(R)c was specifically excluded from joining SOE. The section had strong support from both Churchill and his friend and scientific advisor Professor Lindemann, which ensured it operated in isolation. Although an official name change to MD1 did occur, Churchill's support meant that the unofficial title of 'Winston Churchill's Toyshop' was often adopted due to his preponderance to push through pet projects.

Initially based at 36 Portland Place, the department was forced to move when it was bombed out in the autumn of 1940. They selected a Tudor mansion called the Firs near Aylesbury, where their focus moved from small devices of sabotage to larger-scale problems such as anti-tank weapons.

Polish Government in Exile and Sikorski Statue
47 PORTLAND PLACE

Tube: Regent's Park
Barclays Cycle Hire: Portland Place

The Polish Embassy, where the Polish government in exile were primarily based, can still be found at No. 47, towards the northern end of PORTLAND PLACE.

The Polish government took a torturous path to Britain, first fleeing to Romania, then France and finally on to Britain after the downfall of France, fighting each other almost as much as the Germans along the way.

The Poles had expected to be allowed to pass through Romania on their way to France, not realising that the Germans had already made an agreement with the Romanian government that any Poles entering their country would be interned.

The last acts of the Polish president Ignacy Mościcki, before exile in Romania, were to resign and to name Władysław Raczkiewicz as his replacement. Raczkiewicz's first decision was then to appoint his prime minister, something the French were to have a say in. The French preference was Władysław Sikorski, who had recently been appointed as commander of Polish armed forces, although in somewhat dubious circumstances as it was the Polish ambassador to France who made the appointment. After the fall of Warsaw on 28 September 1939, Raczkiewicz, after two previous suggestions were declined, made Sikorski prime minister.

Eventually the Poles were compelled to leave France for Britain, but that transfer was far from smooth. Sikorski had moved to the front line to take personal command of his troops, so that on 21 June 1940 President Raczkiewicz was met at Paddington station by King George VI without the prime minister.

Eventually Sikorski arrived in London to take up his premiership, but that was by no means the end of the problems dogging the Poles. Determined to divide Sikorski's roles of commander-in-chief of the armed forces and prime minister, Raczkiewicz attempted to install Zaleski as prime minister instead. This led to an armed confrontation at the Polish Embassy at Portland Place

The Polish embassy, scene of an armed standoff between Zaleski and Sikorski; the latter won, leaving Sikorski as the undisputed leader of the Poles.

between the two factions. Eventually Zaleski backed down, leaving Sikorski as the undisputed leader of the Polish government in exile.

Intrigue and politicking seemed to be a feature of the Polish government and followed Sikorski to his death, when on 4 July 1943 his plane crashed on take-off from Gibraltar. Conspiracy theories abounded as to whether the crash was an accident or an assassination, but there is little doubt that with Sikorski's death went much of the influence the Polish government in exile had with its allies. Replaced by Mikołajczyk, the Polish government gradually found itself isolated and very much on the sidelines of political decision-making. As a result, the overthrow of German rule was replaced by Soviet influenced governance that was to last until 1989 with the fall of the Soviet-backed communist regime.

A statue of General Sikorski can be seen opposite the Polish Embassy on the island in the road on Portland Place.

Ed Murrow's Wartime Residence
84 HALLAM STREET

Tube: Great Portland Street
Barclays Cycle Hire: Bolsover Street, Fitzrovia

No. 84 HALLAM STREET can be found just south of the Marylebone Road, parallel to Portland Street, and is near to Regent's Park. The building itself is marked with a blue plaque dedicated to Ed Murrow's residence there.

Ed Murrow was a news reporter for CBS at a time when much of the news received was via the newspapers, with radio still seen as a conduit for entertainment.

From the US, Murrow headed to Britain with his wife Janet as war clouds gathered over Europe. They arrived in 1937 and were to witness the slow creep to war as Hitler reclaimed Austria, annexed the Sudetenland area of Czechoslovakia in 1938 and eventually invaded Poland.

All the while Murrow was reporting back to his listeners in America, but it was not until the chaotic withdrawal from Dunkirk and the onset of the Battle of Britain and then the Blitz that Murrow's talent was to make him a household name.

Murrow was broadcasting to around 15 million listeners back in the USA every night, turning the sights, sounds and fear into ever more descriptive reports that allowed his listeners to understand what the ordinary man and woman in Britain was experiencing.

Throughout the Blitz, Murrow conveyed the daily Luftwaffe raids, but also told a story of ordinary people going about their daily lives, of milk and papers being delivered on time, electricity and gas services working, and of shops still trading despite the bombs that fell every night.

Murrow's broadcasts, which opened with his trademark pause 'This … is London' and ended with his sign off 'Good night and good luck', did much to sway the American public's opinion that they should be involved in the European conflict. Murrow was to become more than just a radio reporter, one among many in London; he was *the* reporter. CBS president William Paley noted the fact he knew everyone and that no door seemed to be closed to him. So respected was Murrow that he was even offered a position as head of the BBC, though he decided it best to decline the offer.

Once his broadcast had finished, Murrow would head back to his flat with a different contingent of reporters and government officials every night, where his wife Janet would have prepared sandwiches. By the end of the war the American ambassador Winant, Eleanor Roosevelt and Mrs Churchill were all to have been entertained in the Murrows' apartment.

The blue plaque adorning 84 Hallam Street where the American broadcaster Ed Murrow lived for the duration of the war.

Murrow was to take his reporting to the war, heading out to North Africa to convey to his listeners the grim reality of the battlefield. He also flew in a Lancaster bomber, *D for Dog*, on a bombing raid over Berlin from which fifty planes and two of the four accompanying reporters failed to return.

Murrow continued to broadcast until the end of the war. He followed the advancing Allies through Normandy, witnessed the troops dropping for the massive airborne operation Market Garden, was there when Buchenwald concentration camp was liberated and moved through Germany with General Patton's Army.

Murrow continued to report on world affairs with simplicity and integrity, but it was the six years of the Second World War and the Blitz of London that first made him such an iconic reporter of the twentieth century. He died of a brain tumour in April 1965.

Mayfair is an area of London roughly bound by Oxford Street to the north, Hyde Park to the west, Regent Street to the east and Piccadilly to the south. Mayfair is one of London's most fashionable districts, with the designer shops of New Bond Street, London's best hotels – the Dorchester and Claridge's – and the US Embassy at its centre in Grosvenor Square.

A great deal of wartime activity focused around the US Embassy, firstly as Britain tried to persuade the US to enter the war and then, once they did, as Britain's closest and most important ally.

In 1938, the US Embassy could be found at 1 Grosvenor Square. As the Lend-Lease programme took off, its offices pitched up at 3 Grosvenor Square, next door. Before long Eisenhower had set up his headquarters on the opposite corner at No. 20 and the Office of Strategic Studies, roughly the equivalent of SOE, had also moved into nearby Grosvenor Street. Soon, high-ranking American officers and liaison staff were moving into the Dorchester, Claridge's and Grosvenor House hotels. Such was the preponderance of American offices that the whole area unsurprisingly acquired the name 'Little America'.

The square itself changed in look as the war went on. The Women's Auxiliary Air Force (WAAF) took over the gardens themselves, where they tended their barrage balloon from their Nissen huts built there. The balloon was, the American ambassador John Winant recalled, nicknamed 'Romeo'. The railings were eventually removed from the perimeter of the gardens for the war effort while other parts of the square were subject to considerable bomb damage.

Despite this, much of the square remains as it was during the war, including the US influence, which is clear to see. The gardens, having previously been private, were opened to the public as part of the 1946 peacetime celebrations and in later years statues of Franklin D. Roosevelt and General Dwight Eisenhower were erected. A more recent memorial, opened in 1995, remembers those who fought with the American-manned Eagle squadrons of the RAF. A blue plaque also marks the building that was Eisenhower's headquarters. With the current, extensive, US Embassy building overlooking Grosvenor Square from the eastern end, Little America lives on.

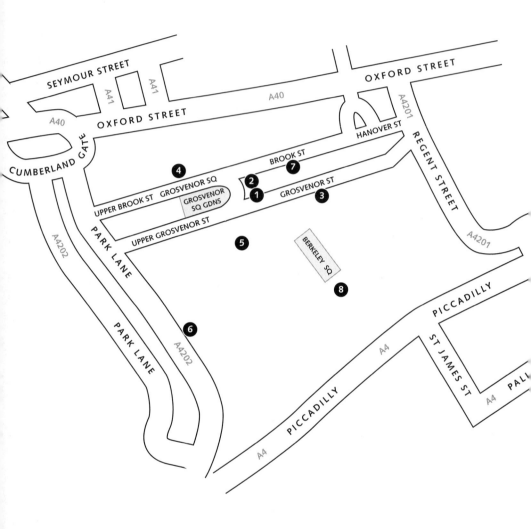

KEY

1. American Embassy
2. US Lend-Lease Mission
3. Office of Strategic Studies
4. Eisenhower's Headquarters
5. The Connaught Hotel
6. The Dorchester Hotel
7. Claridge's Hotel
8. Royal Family Safe House

American Embassy
1 GROSVENOR SQUARE

Tube: Bond Street
Barclays Cycle Hire: Grosvenor Square, Mayfair

From 1938 the US Embassy was at 1 GROSVENOR SQUARE, a grand building on its south-west corner.

In the lead up to war, the American ambassador to the United Kingdom was Joseph Kennedy. Kennedy was a firm proponent of appeasement with Hitler. Believing Britain could not sustain its lone fight against Hitler, his main aim was to keep America out of the European conflict. Having several times advised all Americans to leave the country, Kennedy finally left himself in 1940 to be replaced by the quietly spoken John Gilbert Winant.

Winant made immediate history on his arrival in Britain, being personally greeted by King George VI at Windsor railway station rather than being presented to the king at the palace. As much as anything, this gesture symbolised the desperate times and the need of Britain to bring America into the war. Winant's human touch was to win him over to the British people, from his opening comment to reporters that 'There's no place I'd rather be at this time than in England' to walking around London offering to help where he could, even as the bombs were falling.

Winant believed that the Second World War would eventually be America's war, and that the USA would not be able to stand idly by while Britain was destroyed. As the war dragged on through 1940 and into 1941, Winant continued, in ever more direct words, to counsel America's entry into the conflict. Winant was to prove to be a powerful voice in persuading the president, Franklin D. Roosevelt, to bring America into the war and was a great boon to Churchill and the British government, developing a deep friendship with Anthony Eden, Britain's Foreign Secretary.

Although America did not enter the European war fully until after the attack on Pearl Harbor, the foundations laid by Winant had greatly smoothed over the occasionally thorny relationship between Britain and the US. More importantly, he was instrumental in ensuring the gradual increase of Roosevelt's support for a beleaguered Britain.

With the sudden and fully committed support of American forces, it became abundantly obvious that the British people actually knew very little about their new allies; again Winant recognised the problem and set about changing perceptions. A library was set up in the embassy where a whole range of American literature, from books to magazines, was available for people to read. Winant also hired Wallace Carroll, a former US correspondent

No. 1 Grosvenor Square, home of the US Embassy during the war and now occupied by the Canadian High Commission.

from war-torn London, to head up an American information service which was to inform the British public about everything American.

One curious aside to Winant's time in London was his affair with Sarah Churchill, the prime minister's second eldest daughter. More inclined to stand up to her father, Sarah had embarked on a life on stage and had married, much against her parents' wishes, her fellow performer Vic Oliver. Winant was to meet Sarah on his increasingly regular visits to Chequers, the Churchills' country residence, and began to spend more time with her. Sarah Churchill's marriage was faltering, while Winant's own marriage was a less than happy one and the affair developed. The affair was not, and could probably never have been, a total secret, but their discretion kept it relatively quiet by wartime London's standards.

Winant left Britain in 1947 to return to America, but appeared to become depressed in the post-Second World War world and tragically committed suicide at his home in November that year. The reasoning behind this seemingly out-of-character act will never be known. Britain lost one of its most ardent wartime supporters and a man who unquestionably helped bring about victory.

The US Embassy moved to 24 Grosvenor Square in 1960, where it has the appearance of a fortress, while 1 Grosvenor Square is occupied by the Canadian High Commission.

US Lend-Lease Mission
3 GROSVENOR SQUARE

Tube: Bond Street
Barclays Cycle Hire: Grosvenor Square, Mayfair

No. 3 GROSVENOR SQUARE can be found on the western side of Grosvenor Square, next to what was the US Embassy at 1 Grosvenor Square.

During the war, much of 3 Grosvenor Square was taken up by the American Lend-Lease Mission to the United Kingdom. The Lend-Lease programme was instigated by Roosevelt as a means of helping Britain to stay afloat without need for direct military involvement. When the Lend-Lease Bill was passed by the Senate on 8 March 1941, America itself was not in much of a position to offer military assistance. Although the president decreed that military material should be split equally between the US and Britain, the reality was that the US military was in as great a need as the British. Having been greatly underfunded and poorly run for many years, their active army strength in the autumn of 1939 was 227,000 men compared to Germany's 4 million, and only began its rapid expansion after the Pearl Harbor attack.

The man Roosevelt charged with maintaining the Lend-Lease programme in the UK was Averell Harriman, the heir to the Union Pacific Railroad Company and its chairman at the time of his appointment. Harriman's role was not, at the onset, clearly defined and he found himself caught in between the demands of the British and American governments.

The Lend-Lease programme, while providing much-needed supplies to Britain, was also to cause Roosevelt several problems, first of which was ensuring the aid reached Britain. Roosevelt would not allow American ships to protect the merchantmen, as this was seen as too great a step towards war, so protection was left to the British whose resources were already at breaking point. Although a protected zone was created up to Greenland, where US naval ships patrolled, it did little to stem the flow of aid and military equipment heading to the sea floor.

The political issue with the Lend-Lease programme was the price Britain was made to pay. With little option to hold out for a better deal, Churchill had to accept the terms offered. British gold was shipped directly from South Africa to America, while state-owned companies were sold at knockdown prices, only to be immediately resold for immense profits by the US government. Churchill, and many others in the Cabinet, were furious about the American terms but knew there was little they could do about the situation.

Once in Britain, Harriman found himself with an office in the Admiralty, a weekend guest of Churchill's and beneficiary of no end of classified British intelligence. But, for all that, he was unable to speed up America's inextricable march to war. The introduction of the Lend-Lease programme was taken as a sign by many that America was on the verge of entering the European war, but Harriman knew that it was not an absolute precursor for that step and warned the British not to read it as such. The decisive factor that brought the Americans into the war would prove to be the surprise attack by the Japanese on Pearl Harbor.

For all its intricacies, the Lend-Lease programme was vital to Britain during 1941, when the country was teetering on the verge of defeat. Despite being sold as a way of keeping America out of the European conflict, it also moved the country a step closer to the conflict.

The termination of the Lend-Lease agreement was to stretch relationships further when, eight days after the surrender of Japan, Roosevelt's successor, Harry Truman, cancelled it without warning, sending Britain into a deep food crisis. While the repayment conditions of the loan were generous, with only a tiny proportion to be paid back, there was a string attached. Britain was forced to accept a new economic order that greatly favoured America and the US dollar.

The final instalment of the Lend-Lease debt was paid to America in December 2006. No. 3 Grosvenor Square is now the High Commission of Canada.

Office of Strategic Studies
70 GROSVENOR STREET

Tube: Bond Street
Barclays Cycle Hire: Millennium Hotel, Mayfair

The US Office of Strategic Studies (OSS) was America's first official intelligence agency. Founded in 1942 by William Donovan, it performed broadly similar roles to Britain's Secret Intelligence Service and Special Operations Executive combined.

The OSS London station head was David Bruce, the son-in-law of one of America's top financiers. With shared aims, OSS found itself working very closely with, and learning from, the SIS and SOE. While the OSS were seen, and treated, like the new boys they were to the Great Game, they soon realised that the SIS, still suffering from its pre-war neglect, was not the intelligence agency they were expecting.

As the war moved on, and much to SIS's chagrin, OSS insisted on setting up its own intelligence networks and was soon sending agents into occupied Europe to carry out sabotage and training operations.

The OSS was the forerunner of what is now the Central Intelligence Agency (CIA). Many of its wartime OSS members went on to have illustrious careers there, such as William Casey who became CIA head.

No. 70 Grosvenor Street is now a modern office building.

Eisenhower's Headquarters
20 GROSVENOR SQUARE

Tube: Bond Street
Barclays Cycle Hire: Grosvenor Square, Mayfair

No. 20 GROSVENOR SQUARE can be found diagonally across the gardens in Grosvenor Square from the old US Embassy, and is marked by a blue plaque. This building was occupied by Eisenhower on his arrival in Britain and used as his headquarters.

Eisenhower was working under General Marshall in the War Department in the newly created Operations Division when the decision was made, in April 1942, to launch a cross-Channel invasion. Once returned from this conference, Marshall instructed Eisenhower to lead a team that would make recommendations on how to organise American forces in Great Britain as they

Grosvenor Square Gardens looking across to the Roosevelt memorial and Eisenhower's wartime headquarters.

prepared for the invasion of Nazi-occupied Europe. From this visit Eisenhower submitted a paper to Marshall which detailed the unified command of US forces in Europe: 'Directive for the Commanding General, European Theatre of Operations.' On handing this paper over, Marshall commented to Eisenhower, 'you may be the man who executes it. If that's the case when can you leave?' Three days later Eisenhower was formally advised that he would be the commander of the European Theatre of Operation, United States Army, or ETOUSA. At this point ETOUSA consisted of troops stationed in Iceland and Britain, but the command was created with the sole intention of preparing US forces for the cross-Channel invasion.

By the end of July 1942, Eisenhower was in London, reluctantly travelling to his new headquarters. US Army staff had already moved into the apartment block at 20 Grosvenor Square, but this was certainly not Eisenhower's first choice, as he would have preferred a headquarters outside of a major city. He was forced to accept defeat on this early point primarily as there was nowhere outside of London of sufficient size for their offices. This, combined with the facts that most of the people he would be doing business with were in the centre of London and that transport in and out of the city was shaky, contributed to the decision to remain at 20 Grosvenor Square. With the arrival of so many Americans, the area around Grosvenor Square became known as Little America and then, after Eisenhower's arrival, Eisenhowerplatz.

Eisenhower found his new home difficult and seemed somewhat bemused by the social whirlpool into which he had been thrust. His view was simple: he was there to fight a war, not to be out partying. Consequently he did not accept any invitations except from the armed services or Churchill. Eisenhower did also stay for some time at the Dorchester but, to escape the hotel life, eventually moved to a cottage on the edge of the city.

No. 20 Grosvenor Square remained an important centre of US Army administration throughout the war and has had many uses since, but was undergoing refurbishment at the time of writing.

The Connaught Hotel
CARLOS PLACE

Tube: Bond Street
Barclays Cycle Hire: Millennium Hotel, Mayfair

The Connaught Hotel origins date back to 1815, when it opened as the Prince of Saxe-Coburg Hotel. It underwent expansion and redevelopment and was renamed the Connaught in 1917. It can be found just off Grosvenor Square at CARLOS PLACE.

The Connaught Hotel, de Gaulle's home while in Britain.

Once in Britain, Charles de Gaulle moved into the Connaught, where he remained in residence until the liberation of France. From here he was within easy reach of the Free French Army Headquarters at Carlton Gardens and their counter-espionage unit at Duke Street. Whether it was intentional or not, de Gaulle also found himself close to Eisenhower and the American missions around Grosvenor Square, who gradually took the lead role in the reoccupation of Europe.

While the fighting qualities of the Free French were recognised, as were de Gaulle's leadership skills, his stubbornness prevented him from getting on as well as he may have done with his American neighbours.

The Dorchester Hotel
PARK LANE

Tube: Hyde Park Corner
Barclays Cycle Hire: Stanhope Gate, Mayfair

The Dorchester Hotel, one of London's grandest, can be found on PARK LANE, overlooking Hyde Park, a short walk from Grosvenor Square. The hotel had only been completed nine years before the outbreak of war, a vision of Sir Malcolm Alpine and Sir Francis Towle's to 'create the perfect hotel'.

The Dorchester Hotel was one of the great wartime hotels, along with the Savoy, the Ritz and Claridge's, and was home to many of the leading figures and socialites of the period. Many believed its modern steel and concrete construction made it one of the safest places in London. The heavily sandbagged entrance and air-raid shelters in the basement made all who stayed there feel totally protected from the Luftwaffe's bombs, which by the end of the war had only been able to break a few windows.

The Dorchester, probably above all the other hotels, was the first port of call for those rich enough, or privileged enough, to be able to get accommodation there. Averell Harriman, the US's Lend-Lease administrator and one of the wealthiest men in America, upon arrival in London immediately took up residence in a ground-floor suite at the Dorchester, a short walk from his offices in Grosvenor Square.

Another resident of the Dorchester was Pamela Churchill, Winston Churchill's daughter-in-law by marriage to his eldest son Randolph. With Randolph posted to Egypt, Pamela had taken a job at the Ministry of Supply. Pamela and Harriman inevitably met at the hotel and were soon involved in an intense affair that was kept relatively discreet at first, but soon became public knowledge. The affair was to end in September 1943, when Harriman was made ambassador to the Soviet Union. However, their relationship carried on and off for the next two decades until they finally married in 1971, when Harriman was 78.

Amongst the other guests staying at the hotel were Duff Cooper from the Ministry of Information, Lord Halifax the Foreign Secretary and General Eisenhower, whose suite had a wall built in front of it both for his protection and privacy.

Claridge's Hotel
BROOK STREET

Tube: Bond Street
Barclays Cycle Hire: Grosvenor Square, Mayfair

Claridge's is, without doubt, one of London's finest hotels and can be found on BROOK STREET, a few hundred yards west of Grosvenor Square.

Claridge's started out as a single house hotel, but in an ambitious move, the owners purchased the adjoining five houses and opened as Claridge's in 1856. As its reputation grew, royalty from around the world began to frequent Claridge's and its status as one of London's leading hotels was confirmed. While royalty from Norway and Greece were to stay at the hotel during the war, probably most interesting of all was the royal family of Yugoslavia.

Claridge's Hotel, one of wartime London's most luxurious bolt-holes.

King Peter of Yugoslavia had married Queen Alexandra of Greece at the Yugoslavian Embassy while in exile (see Yugoslavian Embassy, p. 35). She soon fell pregnant and, on 17 July 1945, gave birth to Crown Prince Alexander Karadjordjevic in Suite 212 of Claridge's. This room had, on Churchill's orders, been declared Yugoslavian territory for twenty-four hours to ensure the crown prince was born on Yugoslavian soil.

General Marshall, the Chief of Staff of the US Army from 1939 to 1945, came to London in July 1942 with Admiral King to attend a conference with the British Chiefs of Staff. It had already been decided that it was necessary to launch an offensive operation in 1942, partly for national morale and partly to ease the pressure on the Russian front. It was agreed that the invasion of North Africa, Operation Torch, would be the most profitable line of combined action for the Allied forces, leaving the selection of its commander as the only outstanding decision to be made.

Since it was felt that the invasion of Vichy French North Africa would be more readily accepted if it was perceived as an American operation, the lead role was to go to an American. On 26 July, at his headquarters at Claridge's Hotel, Marshall informed Eisenhower that he was to be the Allied Commander-in-Chief of Operation Torch.

Claridge's remains as one of London's best hotels and in 2012 was undergoing refurbishment.

Royal Family Safe House
FITZMAURICE PLACE

Tube: Green Park
Barclays Cycle Hire: Curzon Street, Mayfair

FITZMAURICE PLACE lies in Mayfair at the northern end of Curzon Street and just south of Berkeley Square.

It was on Fitzmaurice Place that a flat was acquired in great secrecy as a last resort place of retreat for the king and queen, should England have been invaded and London overrun. Fortunately it was never needed and, having only been seen once by the king and queen, it was occupied by the spinster princess sisters, granddaughters of Queen Victoria, Helena and Marie, after their Pall Mall home was bombed.

The area of London known as St James's encapsulates everything south of Piccadilly to Victoria Street and stretches from Buckingham Palace in the west to Whitehall in the east. North of St James's Park you will find St James's Square and Street, and to the south St James's Park Underground station.

St James's, lying right at the heart of London, with the political centre of Whitehall at one end and the royal centre of Buckingham Palace at the other, has been, as might be expected, home to some of the most influential organisations and people within British society.

At the onset of the Second World War, St James's was populated with gentlemen's clubs, where contacts could be made and deals struck. Within society at the time, the club scene was somewhere to entertain guests and to continue business in more relaxed but discreet surroundings. The Carlton Club, affiliated to the Conservative party was located on Pall Mall, until it was bombed out. Boodle's can be found on St James's Street and the oldest club of all, Whites (of which Prince William is a member), can be found on St James's Street. The RAC and Army & Navy clubs, having moved from their original buildings, can be found on Pall Mall.

With the old boys' network being one of, if not the only, way of gaining entry to the secret services, the convenient location of their offices next to 'club land' made for an easy and informal networking arrangement. The Secret Intelligence Services were located south of St James's Park at Broadway, while the Counter-Intelligence Section took over office space on Ryder Street. The newly formed Special Operations Executive came into existence just round the corner from SIS at Caxton Street. The Security Service almost entirely moved out of London early in the war but, obviously feeling a London presence was essential, took up offices in St James's Street, a few minutes' walk from the SIS offices in Ryder Street.

The London Transport Corporation also chose to construct its impressive new offices in St James's, right above the Underground station from where they controlled all of London's public transport networks.

Much power and influence can still be found in St James's today. While the secret services moved on to ever-expanding premises, the Metropolitan Police moved into Broadway where the now famous New Scotland Yard sign rotates in front of their headquarters. Other government departments also occupy buildings around this area, such as the Ministry of Justice, Department for Business, Innovation and Skills and the Attorney General's Office.

A walk along the wide streets of St James's and Pall Mall, then across the park to the contrasting small alleys and twisting streets to the south around the Underground station, will give a fascinating view of London as it was during the war as they are reasonably unchanged.

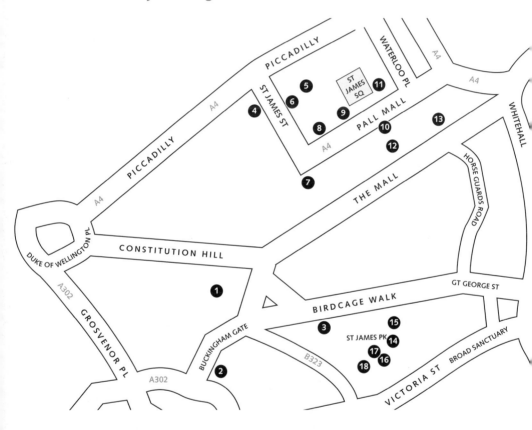

KEY

1. Buckingham Palace
2. The Rubens Hotel
3. Wellington Barracks and the Guards Chapel
4. MI5's London Office
5. SIS, Section V
6. Boodle's
7. St James's Palace
8. Wilkinson Sword & Co.
9. Army & Navy Club
10. The Carlton Club
11. Supreme Headquarters Allied Expeditionary Force
12. Free French Army Headquarters
13. German Embassy
14. London Transport Headquarters
15. SIS Headquarters
16. SIS, D Section
17. St Ermin's Hotel
18. Caxton Hall

Buckingham Palace

ST JAMES'S PARK

Tube: Victoria
Barclays Cycle Hire: Cardinal Place, Victoria

Buckingham Palace, one of London's most famous landmarks, can be found on the western side of ST JAMES'S PARK at the end of the Mall. Buckingham House was bought by George III in 1761 and over time was developed until Queen Victoria became the first sovereign to take up residence there.

In May 1937, King George VI unexpectedly took the throne after Edward VIII abdicated. During the Second World War his palace, along with other great buildings such as St Paul's Cathedral, became a symbol of Britain's defiance in the face of Nazi Germany. The destruction of the palace itself had no strategic importance other than to dent British morale, and it was believed to have been deliberately targeted. With the palace and its grounds covering a vast area of London, it stood out as a prime target and landmark for the Luftwaffe. The palace was bombed at least nine times during the course of the war, with most damage being caused when a stick of six bombs hit the palace grounds (ominously on Friday 13 September 1940), all witnessed by Churchill. Having returned to London from Windsor, finding themselves in the middle of an air raid, Churchill and the queen went to a sitting room overlooking the quadrangle. Churchill recalled hearing 'the zooming noise of

French-Canadian troops outside Buckingham Palace.

a diving aircraft getting louder and louder, and then saw two bombs falling'. Two bombs landed in the quadrangle, one damaging a water main; two fell in the forecourt and one in the garden. The final bomb destroyed the chapel, which was rebuilt after the war as the Queen's Gallery.

Churchill allowed the bombing of the palace to be reported as he rightly judged that the news would boost the nation's morale and resolve. Since the most devastating damage was inflicted on the poorer areas of London, many perceived that the war was targeting them, while leaving the upper classes safe. The bombing of the palace, and its subsequent reporting, helped bridge this divide, leading the queen at the time to comment: 'now I can look the East End in the face.' Despite the intensity of the Blitz, the king and Queen Elizabeth only spent a few nights away from Buckingham Palace.

So expected was the Nazi invasion that the king had a firing range built in the palace gardens so he could practice with assorted weapons, ready to fight off the invaders along with other members of the royal family. However, the invasion never materialised and despite the close calls, Buckingham Palace remained damaged, but standing.

Throughout the war, Buckingham Palace became a refuge for Europe's royalty. Queen Wilhelmina was plucked to safety by a British destroyer and taken to Britain. A few weeks later, King Haakon escaped Norway and spent several months at Buckingham Palace before moving on. On 22 September 1941, a large contingent from Greece arrived in London, including King George II and members of his government, all of whom were welcomed by King George VI.

As the war moved on, the king initiated what were to become traditional Tuesday meetings with Churchill at Buckingham Palace, which changed into lunch, when the two leaders could help themselves from the side. With no servants present, they were able to speak more freely about events and affairs of the war.

Princess Elizabeth, the future queen, made her first wireless broadcast to children of the empire who were in danger or separated from their parents. An Act of Parliament also gave her eligibility to act as one of the counsellors of state who spoke for the king when he was abroad.

A symbolic and lasting accomplishment of George VI was the institution of the George Medal for civilian bravery in 1940. It is estimated that over 32,000 people were awarded the medal personally by George VI, often at the palace, from its inception to the end of the war in 1945. The George Cross also came into being in September 1940 as a direct equivalent to the Victoria Cross, but for actions away from the heat of battle. It could be awarded to civilians or military personnel (or even whole nations, such as the award received by the island of Malta for the population's heroic, and stubborn, refusal to cede defeat in the face of a furious Nazi bombardment). The George Cross could also be awarded retrospectively for actions carried out prior to its investiture, which enabled Flight Lieutenant John Noel Dowland and Leonard Henry Harrison to be properly credited for their actions in defusing bombs on not one, but two ships.

By the end of the war, many of the rooms of the palace were closed, in part because palace staff were leaving to go on active service. With its windows boarded up, it did not look like a grand building by the war's conclusion. Despite this, it was from the palace balcony that Winston Churchill stood, along with the royal family on VE Day, although the king had instructed a careful inspection to make sure it was still sound before their appearance. The balcony had not been used since 1938, when the king stood there with Chamberlain, but even after the mauling the palace had received, it remained sound and was used eight times that day.

The Rubens Hotel
39 BUCKINGHAM PALACE ROAD

Tube: Victoria
Barclays Cycle Hire: Cardinal Place, Victoria

The Rubens Hotel is on BUCKINGHAM PALACE ROAD, opposite the Royal Mews, just on the border of Belgravia and St James.

The Rubens was the hotel used by General Sikorski, leader of the Free Poles, until his untimely death in 1943 (see chapter 3 for more on the Free Poles and General Sikorski).

The plaque on the Rubens Hotel reminds guests of the Polish general's wartime presence.

Wellington Barracks and the Guards Chapel
BIRDCAGE WALK

Tube: St James's Park
Barclays Cycle Hire: Butler Place, Westminster

Wellington Barracks is the home of the Foot Guards and can be found overlooking St James's Park only a few minutes' walk from Buckingham Palace. The Guards Division is formed by Grenadiers, Coldstream, Scots, Irish and Welsh Guards. Along with the Household Cavalry, they make up the Household Division.

An airborne assault on Whitehall was anticipated as part of the expected German invasion of Britain. Being located so close to Whitehall, the Grenadier Guards were assigned to its defence and were ready to rush from their barracks should any enemy soldiers appear.

The Guards Chapel, next to Wellington Barracks, was originally built in 1838 and supports the Household Division. On 18 June 1944, just five days after the first V1 flying bomb struck London, another V1 hit the church, killing 121 servicemen and civilians and destroying the building. Legend has it that the altar candles remained alight. It took several days to dig all the victims out of the rubble and little of the church remained. It was rebuilt in the 1960s around the original apse, which was one of the few parts to survive.

The post-war Ferret armoured car, on display outside the Guard's Chapel on Birdcage Walk.

MI5's London Office
57–58 ST JAMES'S STREET

Tube: Green Park
Barclays Cycle Hire: Green Park Station, West End

ST JAMES'S STREET can be found at the end of Pall Mall, heading north from St James's Palace, with Nos 57–58 being at the northern end nearest Piccadilly.

When MI5 left Wormwood Scrubs and headed to the country estate of Blenheim Palace, they did not abandon London entirely. Their London presence was at 57–58 St James's Street, not far from the Secret Intelligence Services building on Broadway. This London office allowed MI5 to liaise with other London-based departments.

One of the main sections of MI5 to be found in London was B1A, which ran the most successful double-cross system of the war. While Section B1A was responsible for the day-to-day running of the operation, the Twenty Committee (or XX Committee) was responsible for its overall strategy. They met every Thursday at MI5's St James's Street offices. The committee's chairman was an Oxford don John Masterman, who equated the whole process to running a cricket team.

The double-cross spy ring was conceived and developed by Thomas 'Tar' Robertson and was spectacularly successful. The Nazi secret service, the Abwehr, turned out to be fairly inept when it came to placing agents in Britain; MI5 were confident that all those sent in were captured. Some of these would-be German agents were to work for the British as double agents;

St James's Street, MI5's London office after it was bombed out of Wormwood Scrubs prison.

pretending their mission was going to plan, they were to feed false information back across the Channel. The other, more precious, spies were those who actively travelled between countries, meeting their German handlers, plying them with the misinformation supplied by the British. One of the first was Dusko Popov, a Serbian businessman whose travel between London and Lisbon allowed him not only to gain information from his 'contacts' in London, but also to pass on the information to his German handlers.

With Popov's credentials secured, he was given the new code name Tricycle (on account of his preference for three-in-a-bed sex) and furnished with offices on Regent Street as cover for his newly formed company.

The whole double-cross programme orchestrated by Tar Robertson was to be used to conceal the true objective of the D-Day landings. Everyone knew a cross-Channel invasion was coming, though the Germans assumed it would target the Pas de Calais, not Normandy. Operation Fortitude was the deception plan that was to ensure that they never questioned this assumption.

The double-cross spies, Tricycle, Bronx, Brutus, Garbo and Treasure, were to feed the Abwehr such a wealth of convincing yet false information that several days after the D-Day landings Garbo was still able to convince the Germans that the attack was diversionary and the real blow was yet to come at the Pas de Calais.

Secret Intelligence Service, Section V
RYDER STREET

Tube: Green Park
Barclays Cycle Hire: Green Park Station, West End

RYDER STREET can be found just off St James's Street (where the wartime MI5 offices were to be found) and is almost exactly halfway up on the right-hand side as you head towards Piccadilly.

Section V, the Counter-Intelligence (or Security) Section of SIS was responsible for counter-espionage and was to grow from just three officers prior to the outbreak of the war to 163 officers by the time the war ended in 1945. They moved from their Victorian house in St Albans into their Ryder Street offices part way through the war.

Section V was hunting out threats to the country's secret intelligence, similar to that of MI5's B Division, where B1A was running the successful double-cross programme. As such, there were suggestions that Section V and B Division should be merged. This was not a proposal that was going to be universally accepted, with MI5 officers feeling that SIS was treading on their toes by interfering in work that was their 'principal concern', while SIS failed to see how the home branch of the intelligence service could carry out counter-espionage operations abroad. In reality, the two sections did work together, with MI5 substantively assisting Section V's development as they expanded at the beginning of the war. Also, once Section V had moved into its Ryder Street offices, the two departments were to be physically close, further enhancing their relationship. Section V operated throughout the war gathering counter-intelligence information from agents in the field and Ultra sources, and passing it on to other parties.

Section V was to have one major problem: unbeknown to anyone at the time, the head of their Iberian Section was the Russian spy Kim Philby. Philby was much trusted in SIS, and his influence was wide ranging. The Americans set up the Office of Strategic Studies (see OSS at Grosvenor Street, p. 62) in 1942, principally to provide the same services provided by SIS. One of its young stars was James Jesus Angleton, who was to work for the OSS Counter-Espionage (X-2) Branch, located in the same Ryder Street building as Section V. Angleton, who was to become the CIA's counter-intelligence chief for twenty years, was greatly influenced by Philby when they worked together at this time. It is hard to determine whether Philby did any harm to the Allied cause during the war years, since he was as committed to the destruction of National Socialism as much as he was committed to the Soviet cause. The damage he caused in the years after the war is immeasurable; unbelievably, he was not confirmed as a Soviet agent until his defection in 1963.

Boodle's
28 ST JAMES'S STREET

Tube: Green Park
Barclays Cycle Hire: Green Park Station, West End

Boodle's, the second oldest club after Whites, can be found at 28 ST JAMES'S STREET, just north of Ryder Street, and was just around the corner from SIS Counter-Intelligence Section on Ryder Street.

Many important people belonged to this club, but it is especially worthy of mention as two of the most well-known people from Second World War history were members: Winston Churchill and Ian Fleming.

Boodle's is still very much in operation today and has changed little since its founding in 1762, although it did begin to admit women members after much debate.

St James's Palace
MARLBOROUGH ROAD

Tube: Green Park
Barclays Cycle Hire: St James's Square, St James's

St James's Palace can be found at the junction of Pall Mall, MARLBOROUGH ROAD and St James's Street, conspicuous as the Foot Guards with their bearskins stand on duty at the gates. Built by Henry VIII around 1535, St James's Palace remains as the official residence of the sovereign, although since Queen Victoria's reign, Buckingham Palace has taken over as the main place of residence.

During the war, like many important buildings, guard duties were often taken up by the Home Guard while regular forces were deployed out of the country or were located in more strategically important roles. As the regular forces became stretched, the Home Guard took over much of St James's Palace guard duties.

St James's Palace was also witness to the beginning of one of the defining post-war organisations: the United Nations. On 12 June 1941, while victory was still far from certain in the eyes of many, the exiled governments of Europe and representatives from the Commonwealth and Great Britain signed

St James's Palace today, showing how little has changed since the Second World War.

St James's Palace with a member of the Home Guard. They had taken on sentry duties from regular soldiers who were deployed to combat roles. © TfL from the London Transport Museum

the 'declaration of St James's Palace'. This is seen as the first commitment to develop the organisation that was to become the United Nations with the words: 'The only true basis of enduring peace is the willing cooperation of free peoples in a world in which, relieved of the menace of aggression, all may enjoy economic and social security. It is our intention to work together, and with other free peoples, both in war and peace, to this end.'

St James's Palace is still at the heart of the royal household and many important offices, associated with the daily running of the royal household, can be found there, such as those of Prince William and Prince Harry.

Wilkinson Sword & Co.
53 PALL MALL

Tube: Green Park
Barclays Cycle Hire: Waterloo Place, St James's

Wilkinson Sword & Co. were manufacturers of swords and bayonets for the military and had a London office at the western end of PALL MALL, towards St James's Palace. It was at this office that one of the most curious but relatively unknown meetings of the Second World War took place.

Wilkinson Sword & Co.'s London office, where the Fairbairn-Sykes fighting knife, still used by the Royal Marines, was conceived.

Churchill had ordered the creation of the commandos, his 'iron fist from the sea'. It was envisaged that the commandos would carry out lightning raids on German targets. However, it was quickly seen that there was a need for a dedicated fighting knife for both close-quarters combat and dealing with unfortunate enemy soldiers with stealth and in silence. Such a knife was something the British did not have, as the standard-issue bayonet was unsuitable due to its size and shape. Captain Leslie Wood of SOE sought to recruit experts in unarmed combat and knife fighting. The men he found were Fairbairn and Sykes from the Shanghai police department where they had learnt the dark arts of gutter fighting.

The pair met with Wilkinson Latham of Wilkinson Sword at their Pall Mall office in November 1940 to discuss the characteristics of a fighting knife, at one point acting out a knife fight using a ruler to demonstrate their point. By the end of the meeting the first design of what was to become the Fairbairn-Sykes (or simply F-S) fighting knife had been created. Shortly after this meeting, on 14 November 1940, Captain Leslie Wood placed the first order for 1,500 F-S fighting knives with Wilkinson Sword.

Wilkinson Sword were active in the manufacture of weapons throughout the Second World War, but also created ceremonial swords. The most famous of these was the Stalingrad Sword that was presented by Churchill to Stalin to commemorate the Russian victory at that city. It can now be seen on display at the Battle of Stalingrad Museum in Volgograd.

Army & Navy Club
36 PALL MALL

Tube: Charing Cross
Barclays Cycle Hire: Waterloo Place, St James's

The Army & Navy Club, also known as 'The Rag', was founded in 1837 and has been at its current PALL MALL location since 1851. It underwent a complete refurbishment in 1962.

The Army & Navy Club's address was used on correspondence to a fictional person, Major W. Martin, the name given to the body dropped in Operation Mincemeat, which was the plan to deceive the Nazis of the true intentions of the attack on Scilly (see St Pancras Coroner's Office p. 116 and Hackney Mortuary p. 119).

Amongst the other papers secreted about his person was a letter addressed to 'Major Martin' at the 'Army and Navy Club, Pall Mall' from Lloyds Bank, asking him to settle a '£79.19s. 2d overdraft'.

The Carlton Club
100 PALL MALL

Tube: Charing Cross
Barclays Cycle Hire: Waterloo Place, St James's

The Carlton Club, like many others, was founded along political lines, in this case by several Tory MPs after their party's defeat by the Reforming Party in 1831. The club soon outgrew its original building and moved to new premises on PALL MALL, where it remained until the intervention of a German high-explosive bomb.

On 14 October the single bomb hit, and virtually destroyed, the building, reducing much of it to rubble and leaving the remainder ablaze. This was witnessed from atop of the No. 10 Annex by Churchill, from where he observed that 'the greater part of Pall Mall was in flames'.

On finding the chief whip, Captain David Margesson, the miraculous turn of events was revealed to Churchill. The building had around 250 people in it when the bomb hit, but they all managed to escape from the rubble

The rather plain building that replaced the destroyed Carlton Club at 100 Pall Mall.

alive, with Quintin Hogg carrying his father out of the ruins. Margesson, who usually slept at the club, was found a spare bed in the basement of the Annex, no doubt pondering his lucky escape and the destruction of his car which had been flattened by the falling building.

The club immediately moved to 69 St James's Street, opposite King Street, where it remains to this day. It is clearly marked with blue railings and lampposts, and is still affiliated to the Conservative party.

Supreme Headquarters Allied Expeditionary Force
31 ST JAMES'S SQUARE

Tube: Charing Cross
Barclays Cycle Hire: St James's Square, St James's

ST JAMES'S SQUARE is just off the east end of Pall Mall, with No. 31 in the bottom right corner of the square.

When Eisenhower was appointed commander-in-chief (C-in-C) of Operation Torch, the invasion of North Africa, it was certain that he would lead the cross-Channel invasion. Eisenhower was informed by Roosevelt that he was going to command Operation Overlord in early December 1943. Operation Overlord was the codename for the assault on mainland Europe by the multinational Allied forces. By the middle of January 1944 Eisenhower was back in London as the supreme commander of Overlord. SHAEF, the Supreme Headquarters Allied Expeditionary Force, was the military headquarters dedicated to planning and directing that attack. The major part of this organisation was located outside of London, on Eisenhower's insistence, at Bushey Park, while the London section could be found at 31 St James's Square.

It was during the difficult African and Italian campaigns that Eisenhower developed his techniques for dealing with large multinational formations under a single command. Ultimately, when he began adding further men to his command structure, many had proven themselves under his command previously, and any he thought not suited to the Allied command structure had been weeded out. One of Eisenhower's first tasks as C-in-C of Overlord

The SHAEF headquarters on St James's Square is marked by not one but two commemorative plaques.

was to appoint his direct subordinates, the men who would direct different elements of the war. Air Chief Marshal Sir Arthur Tedder was appointed as Deputy Supreme Allied Commander while Air Marshal Sir Trafford Leigh-Mallory became Air Forces Commander and Admiral Sir Bertram Ramsay Naval Forces Commander. Field Marshal Bernard Montgomery, Lieutenant General Omar Bradley and Lieutenant General Jacob Devers were all appointed Ground Forces Commanders.

The planning for the cross-Channel invasion had been ongoing for many years under the guidance of Lieutenant General Frederick Morgan. Although he was never going to lead the invasion, Morgan and his staff had collected all the detail necessary to make D-Day happen, such as preliminary plans and supply estimates. Once Eisenhower took up his post, he was able to expand on the Overlord plan created by Morgan and carry it into effect. Montgomery was made, as Eisenhower called it, the 'battle-line commander' for the opening attack and the build-up of forces on the Normandy coast until the breakout began. In this capacity he led much of the planning and refinement of Morgan's plans, primary of which was to enlarge the attack from three divisions to five.

Operation Overlord was put into effect with D-Day being delayed until 6 June 1944. Despite strong resistance, the Allied forces were able to carry the attack forward and create a foothold on mainland Europe, from which they would advance into the heart of Nazi Germany.

While much of this success was down to the bravery of the men on the ground, it is without doubt that the meticulous plans set out in this building ensured that those soldiers were trained, equipped and supplied with all they needed for this vast undertaking.

By December 1944, SHAEF had established itself in the Trianon Palace Hotel in Versailles, France, and in April 1945 it moved to Frankfurt.

Free French Army Headquarters
4 CARLTON GARDENS

Tube: Charing Cross
Barclays Cycle Hire: Waterloo Place, St James's

Charles de Gaulle's headquarters while in exile were located at 4 CARLTON GARDENS and is marked by the presence of several plaques. A statue of de Gaulle can be seen opposite 4 Carlton Gardens.

At the outbreak of the Second World War, de Gaulle was a colonel in the French Army, in which he commanded the 4th Armoured Division. Despite distinguishing himself in combat, it was impossible to hold back the German advance into France. De Gaulle was provisionally promoted to

The statue of Charles de Gaulle overlooking St James's Park. De Gaulle was a divisive figure, inspiring both respect and resentment.

brigadier general and then, as the French collapse continued, he was given the role of Undersecretary of State for National Defence and War by Prime Minister Paul Reynaud.

On 16 June 1940, refusing to accept the decision to surrender taken by Pétain (the French premier who supplanted Reynaud), de Gaulle was spirited out of France by Churchill's military advisor in France, Edward Spears. A few days later, on 18 June 1940, in his famous BBC radio broadcast, he called on the French people to resist the German occupation. He also created the Free French movement, uniting their forces that had escaped and claiming sovereignty over France.

De Gaulle was an effective leader of the Free French during the years of occupation by the Nazis and governance by Pétain in Vichy France. He proved to possess the necessary qualities required to lead and motivate the French troops and peoples, scattered around Britain and the world, after their defeat. However, his continual demands led to some resentment from other leaders, most notably Eisenhower, whom de Gaulle refused to serve under as he was not French.

De Gaulle left for France at the earliest opportunity after D-Day, and then moved to Paris as soon as it was liberated, taking over leadership of the country.

German Embassy
8–9 CARLTON HOUSE TERRACE

Tube: Charing Cross
Barclays Cycle Hire: Waterloo Place, St James's

The German Embassy in London, from 1849 up until the outbreak of the Second World War, could be found at 8–9 CARLTON HOUSE TERRACE.

The ambassador appointed by Hitler was Joachim von Ribbentrop, who took up his duties in October 1936, but he was destined to leave in early 1938 to take up the role of Foreign Minister. Von Ribbentrop's replacement was Herbert von Dirksen.

Von Dirksen fought in the First World War before becoming a career politician, occupying a range of postings in the German Foreign Office. He eventually became Germany's ambassador to Japan from 1933 until he was transferred to London briefly before the outbreak of war.

On 1 September 1939 Germany invaded Poland and at 11.15 a.m. two days later, Chamberlain announced that Britain was at war with Germany.

This building was the German Embassy up until Britain's declaration of war on Germany.

The German Embassy was closed and von Dirksen's brief tenure ended as he returned home to relative obscurity. He escaped any punishment at the Nuremburg Trials and went on to write up his memoirs in 1951. He died in 1955.

After the building was vacated by the Germans it was used by the Foreign Office up until the mid-1960s.

London Transport Headquarters
55 BROADWAY

Tube: St James's Park
Barclays Cycle Hire: Abbey Orchard Street, Westminster

London Transport's headquarters can be found at 55 BROADWAY, directly above St James's Park Underground station. The building was commissioned in the 1920s and was the highest office building in London at the time, standing at 174ft. These offices are still used by London Transport today.

The London Transport Offices, located above St James's Underground station on Broadway, showing the bomb-damaged west wing. © TfL from the London Transport Museum

The transport network around London was controlled by the London Transport Passenger Board (LTPB) and was responsible for all trains, buses and trams in the London area. As the Blitz steadily intensified, so did the damage to London's transport network that was so vital for the effective running of the city. Many Tube stations were damaged or destroyed, some like Balham with great loss of life. Depots were also hit, while buses seemed to end up in the firing line with alarming regularity. Throughout this chaos, the LTPB were to maintain functioning transport services, even if there were delays caused by destroyed railway lines, damaged roads and wrecked rolling stock.

The running of London's transport network was not made any easier when the LTPB offices were damaged: the entire west wing of the Broadway building was gutted by Luftwaffe bombs. However, the transport network continued to operate.

The building was fully restored after the war and continues to operate as the main administration centre of London Transport.

Secret Intelligence Service Headquarters
54 BROADWAY

Tube: St James's Park
Barclays Cycle Hire: Abbey Orchard Street, Westminster

No. 54 BROADWAY can be found opposite St James's Park Underground station, and is next door to the Old Star Pub which was plying its trade there when SIS moved in. Broadway is just south of St James's Park and can be reached by crossing Birdcage Walk and going through one of the passageways into Queen Anne's Gate.

The Secret Intelligence Service (SIS), colloquially known as MI6, has been in existence since 1909. SIS is responsible for the gathering of all intelligence from foreign sources and is answerable to the Foreign Office (see FCO, p. 104).

SIS moved into 54 Broadway, along with the Government Code & Cypher School (GC&CS, who were responsible during the Second World War for the famous Enigma decrypts) in 1926, although it was not until just before the start of the Second World War that SIS had expanded sufficiently to occupy the entire building. When the Passport Control Office moved into the building behind the SIS offices at 21 Queen Anne's Gate, a secret passageway was built joining the two to keep any link between them secret.

Shortly after the commencement of hostilities with Germany an inauspicious change in head was forced on SIS when their current 'C', Admiral Sir Hugh Sinclair, died of cancer of the spleen in early November 1939. His successor, Colonel Stewart Menzies, was eventually installed as the new 'C'

The rather innocent-looking offices of MI6 at 54 Broadway. MI6 was put under immense pressure to gather intelligence on the Axis nations.

on 28 November 1939. Even as Sinclair's de facto deputy and with Sinclair's recommendation, old rivalries played out which delayed his appointment and nearly prevented him from getting the job. Even Churchill, in his capacity as First Lord of the Admiralty, tried to influence the outcome, suggesting his own naval candidate.

During the 1930s, as the world edged ever closer to conflict, SIS was increasingly being told it needed to glean information on hostile nations', especially Germany's, intentions. Sinclair had evidently been making progress since the Nazis came to power in 1933, but the whole dynamic changed when Poland was invaded. Long-term intelligence, while of political and military value, was not what the armed forces required. They needed tactical information on what the enemy intended to do that day or the next.

While agent networks were useful, SIS had the most marked success with the GC&CS decrypts of German Enigma coded transmissions. The Nazis' radio traffic was encoded by Enigma cipher machines, and the Luftwaffe, Abwehr, Army and Navy all had slightly different variants that were believed by the Germans to be unbreakable. In preparation for war, MI6 had moved the GC&CS up to Bletchley Park, where an eclectic mix of university dons, eccentrics and geniuses such as Alan Turing broke the codes and provided the famous Ultra material, the code name for all information emanating out of Bletchley Park.

SIS was to remain in their Broadway offices until they moved to Century House, Lambeth, in 1964. The building is now used as offices.

Secret Intelligence Service, D Section
2 CAXTON STREET, ST JAMES'S

Tube: St James's Park
Barclays Cycle Hire: Butler Place, Westminster

No. 2 CAXTON STREET, home to D Section (also known as Section IX) of SIS, can be found on the corner of Broadway and is just around the corner from MI6's then main office building at 54 Broadway.

Set up in 1938 by the then chief of SIS, Admiral Sir Hugh Sinclair, with Major Laurence Grand as its head, D Section was to be responsible for the planning and implementation of clandestine operations. This was a significant move for MI6, which was an organisation that lived in the shadows and avoided the spectacular wholesale destruction being proposed.

No. 2 Caxton Street where the SOE adventure to 'set Europe ablaze' began.

Initially, since Britain was not yet at war, D Section's task was to plan and prepare for possible operations in an occupied country. Lists of targets were drawn up along with the proposed means to carry out the attacks. Obvious infrastructure was chosen, such as factories and power stations, but Grand's section were also more inventive, suggesting the 'adulteration of food supplies and agriculture by the introduction of pests to crops and diseases to animals'.

Such planning also had another side effect: the British had to consider the possibility that the Germans were preparing the same kinds of attack and that Britain must develop its defences.

In July 1940, the Special Operations Executive was formed, into which D Section was logically included. By an incredible clerical error, Menzies (the new chief of MI6) was not notified for several weeks that D Section had officially left his organisation. Dalton, as the minister in charge of SOE, then had to face the issue of whom to place in charge of SOE, Sir Frank Nelson or Grand from D Section. Nelson was installed as the chief of SOE and as a result Grand was removed from D Section to return to his career as a military engineer.

The Caxton Street offices were rapidly filled up by the ever-expanding SOE and spilled over into the St Ermin's Hotel next door, but this was soon full and alternative accommodation was sought. In October 1940, SOE began their move from Caxton Street to their permanent wartime offices at 64 Baker Street.

No. 2 Caxton Street is now an upmarket restaurant, the Caxton Grill, which is part of St Ermin's Hotel.

St Ermin's Hotel
CAXTON STREET

Tube: St James's Park
Barclays Cycle Hire: Butler Place, Westminster

In 1939 St Ermin's Hotel was, as it is now, a smart London hotel. Its entrance is set back from the road in between 2 CAXTON STREET to the right and Caxton Hall to the left.

As the number of people joining SOE swelled its ranks, any free space in the old D Section offices at 2 Caxton Street was soon used up. The first phase of expansion moved some SOE staff into the fourth floor of the hotel. This arrangement with staff at 2 Caxton Street and St Ermin's soon became too difficult to manage, especially as the organisation was still growing. As a result, the vast majority of SOE moved into their famous Baker Street offices in 1940.

Caxton Hall
10 CAXTON STREET

Tube: St James's Park
Barclays Cycle Hire: Butler Place, Westminster

Caxton Hall dates back to the 1880s, when it was a Westminster Town Hall. It can be found in CAXTON STREET, which is a few hundred yards from St James's Park Underground station, opposite New Scotland Yard.

During the late 1930s and early 1940s, Churchill gave speeches and held press conferences here which have been commemorated by a green plaque prominently placed on the building.

Another more infamous episode that occurred at Caxton Hall was the assassination by Udam Singh of Michael O'Dwyer in March 1940. O'Dwyer had been governor of Punjab when the Amritsar massacre took place, in which hundreds of unarmed Indians were shot by British troops. As governor at the time, Singh held O'Dwyer responsible for the massacre and had waited twenty years to exact his revenge. While Singh was sent to the gallows, Nazi propaganda apparently tried to use the incident to incite rebellious factions in India.

Caxton Hall has since been turned into expensive residential apartments.

Caxton Hall, where Churchill gave many speeches, and where Udam Singh assassinated Michael O'Dwyer – an event the Nazi propaganda machine tried to capitalise on.

In 1529, after Cardinal Wolsey's downfall, Henry VIII seized the whole Whitehall area for his own personal use, with the buildings there forming the basis of Whitehall Palace, so called because of the white stone that had been used. A fire in 1698 destroyed much of the area, and with St James's Palace becoming the sovereign's official residence, grand townhouses were built on the Whitehall Palace site. Government offices soon started to dominate the area, with Downing Street becoming the official residence of the prime minister.

As the spectre of war loomed, Whitehall, with the Houses of Parliament at its southern end, now presented Britain's central government as one concentrated target. Virtually every building along Whitehall and in the surrounding area was a government office. The occupation by expanding government departments, as the War Office requisitioned buildings in the immediate vicinity, significantly increased the target area.

Throughout the 1930s, as war became an increasing possibility, the basements of the Whitehall buildings were strengthened to provide protection against air raids. The terrifying prospect of total destruction from the air was envisaged by government officials based on figures extrapolated from the casualties from the First World War Zeppelin raids.

Plans were made to remove the seat of government from London entirely, with some departments moving to Harrogate and Bath, and plans were made for a full evacuation from London of all ministers and other government officials. The Cabinet War Rooms were also constructed, mainly for temporary use until the entire government operation had been evacuated. In the event, the Nazi invasion of Poland was not immediately followed up by the massive, destructive air raids envisioned and a reasonable level of normality was maintained. Even at the height of the Blitz, while extensive, the casualties and damage was much lower than many predictions. However, the threat of invasion still loomed. Even with the rescue of the British Expeditionary Force (BEF) from Dunkirk, it was still widely felt that it was not a question of 'will Britain be invaded' but 'when will Britain be invaded?'

With Churchill now in Downing Street, it was considered a real possibility that Whitehall itself could be subject to a lightning German attack by paratroopers with the sole purpose of

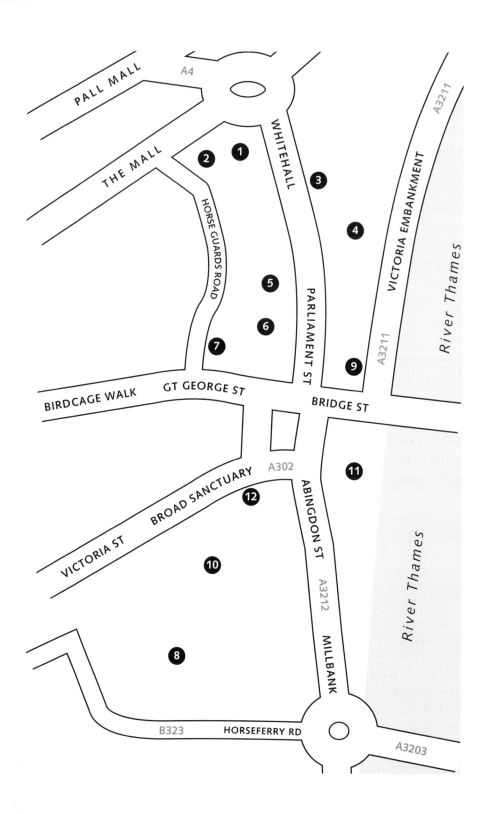

destroying Britain's centre of governance. General Ismay, Chief of Staff to the Minister of Defence and Deputy Secretary to the War Cabinet, was put in charge of organising these defences and drew up detailed plans to defend the area to the last man. Even Churchill himself had no intention of leaving, vowing to die fighting the enemy.

Ismay's plans involved soldiers creating roadblocks, lining rooftops, manning sandbag pillboxes and occupying buildings in a plan designed to turn Whitehall into a last redoubt. The thought of positioning British soldiers on top of Admiralty Arch so they could fire on to advancing enemy infantry in Trafalgar Square must have been sobering. The loopholes in the newly built Admiralty citadel can still be seen today, though the pillbox disguised as a W.H. Smith bookstand in Parliament Square sadly does not.

Whitehall was hit by several bombs during the war but, apart from the direct hit to the Houses of Parliament, few others caused serious damage and Churchill and his government were able to remain in Whitehall for the duration of the war.

When Nazi Germany finally surrendered, Whitehall was the scene of much of the celebration. Massive crowds gathered to see and cheer Churchill as victory was announced. On telling the crowd it was 'your victory' they replied as one to Churchill, 'no, it's yours'.

KEY

1. Admiralty
2. Admiralty Citadel
3. War Office
4. MoD Main Building
5. 10 Downing Street
6. Foreign and Commonwealth Office
7. Cabinet War Rooms and No. 10 Annex
8. The Rotundas
9. New Scotland Yard
10. Church House
11. Palace of Westminster
12. Westminster Abbey

Admiralty
OLD ADMIRALTY BUILDING, SPRING GARDENS

Tube: Charing Cross
Barclays Cycle Hire: Craven Street, Strand

The building now known as the 'Old Admiralty Building' can be found at the top of Whitehall, close to Trafalgar Square. The Old Admiralty Building, as the name suggests, was built to house the Admiralty: the single body in charge of the Royal Navy up until 1964, when they were combined with the War Office to form the Ministry of Defence. Admiralty Arch which spans the Mall is linked to the Old Admiralty Building by a passageway and was damaged during an air raid.

The Admiralty was the operational headquarters of the Royal Navy (RN) at all levels, with the fleet being its prime concern. The RN is controlled by the Board of Admiralty, which consists of high-ranking naval officers with ministerial oversight in the form of the First Lord of the Admiralty, who was effectively the head of the group. On 3 September 1939, the day Britain declared war on Germany, Chamberlain offered Churchill the position of the First Lord of the Admiralty and a place in the War Cabinet. Churchill commented on this in his war diaries: 'Had the Prime Minister in the first instance given me the choice between the War Cabinet and the Admiralty, I should of course have chosen the Admiralty. Now I was to have both.'

Churchill wasted no time in getting to grips with the job he had left a quarter of a century before, telling the Admiralty that he would be there at six that evening, meeting the First Sea Lord Admiral Pound and the other sea lords. For their part, the Admiralty sent a signal to the fleet that simply said, 'Winston is back.'

The British Fleet was substantial, far eclipsing the power of the German Kriegsmarine, comprising over 500 ships and boats of all classes. Of these, there were 7 aircraft carriers, 12 battleships, 3 pocket battleships and 184 destroyers. The submarine strengths were comparable at the outbreak of war, with the Royal Navy having fifty-eight and the Kriegsmarine fifty-seven, but the Germans were to use their U-boats with devastating effect to try to starve Britain of its vital supplies in the Battle of the Atlantic. Also, the Germans were to complete the construction of another fifty-eight boats by the end of 1940.

The Admiralty's tasks were wide ranging, covering all forms of naval warfare, from the safe passage of the merchant navy to dealing with German mine laying around the British coast and the delivery of reinforcements to battered British units. The phoney war was not so inactive for sailors in the Royal Navy, who were involved in some of the first confrontations with the enemy, registering some spectacular triumphs and defeats. German U-boats

The London victory parade, celebrating the defeat of the Axis forces, passes through Admiralty Arch, 8 June 1946. © TfL from the London Transport Museum

were to score some early victories, notably the sinking of HMS *Royal Oak* by *U-47*, which entered the anchorage at Scapa Flow. This was followed by the sinking of the aircraft carrier HMS *Courageous* in the Western Approaches by *U-29*. However, the Royal Navy were to hit back, critically damaging the German pocket battleship *Admiral Graf Spee* at River Plate; the ship was scuttled shortly after.

One of the RN's greatest achievements of the early stages of the war was Operation Dynamo, the extraction of over 300,000 British and French troops from Dunkirk in May and June 1940, masterminded by Vice Admiral Bertram Ramsay. Although the navy and the little ships paid a heavy toll, the men rescued enabled Britain to fight on.

Linked to the Admiralty building is Admiralty House, the official residence of the First Lord of the Admiralty. The building is now split into grace-and-favour flats leased rent-free to senior Cabinet ministers, but was occupied by Churchill from 1939. Throughout the war Churchill used Admiralty House where he had a private cinema in the basement to watch everything from wartime dramas to the latest Disney pictures.

The Old Admiralty Building is now home to the UK Foreign and Commonwealth Office.

Admiralty Citadel
SPRING GARDENS

Tube: Charing Cross
Barclays Cycle Hire: Craven Street, Strand

The Admiralty citadel can be found on the corner of the Old Admiralty Building, overlooking Horse Guards. It stands out due to its nature as a modern-day castle and is almost certainly the most unattractive building in all of Whitehall. The building stands, absurdly placed, among the fine Whitehall architecture and, although attempts have been made to soften the building's appearance with creepers, they do not detract from the loopholes, gun emplacements and brutally functional nature of the structure.

The Admiralty citadel was not completed until after the major bombing raids of the Blitz. It was designed to allow the RN intelligence division to continue to operate through the Luftwaffe air assault that was expected to continue and decimate the city of London, making it impossible to run the war effort from the existing Whitehall offices.

The back of the beautiful Old Admiralty Building, with the imposing Admiralty citadel to its left; unfortunately there was little time to work on the aesthetics.

The building was also designed to be used as a last line of defence against any Nazi assault. It was still widely anticipated that Britain would be invaded, and the possibility of a surprise attack on Whitehall by paratroopers was considered a very real threat.

While Churchill thought the demolition of the structure would be a task for future generations, it has remained and is still believed to be in use by the RN to this day.

War Office
OLD WAR OFFICE, WHITEHALL

Tube: Embankment
Barclays Cycle Hire: Whitehall Place, Strand

The building that is now referred to as the Old War Office lies on the east side of WHITEHALL. The original War Offices were on the south side of Pall Mall and were a collection of adjoining houses with knocked-through doorways. A new War Office was proposed as far back as the 1860s, but the digging of the foundations was not to start until 1899, with the War Office officially opening in 1906.

The War Office was both a department of state and a military headquarters. It was home to the Secretary of State for War and the Chief of the Imperial General Staff. On the outbreak of the Second World War, the War Office began a massive expansion that probably exceeded a similar type of expansion in 1914, when the War Office occupied, or partly occupied, fifty-two buildings around London. Many of the grand hotels around Whitehall were rapidly requisitioned, with the Victoria, Metropole and others quickly being occupied by War Office staff (see entries on pp. 128 & 129 for further details).

The Secretary of State for War or Defence Secretary occupied the impressive Haldane Room, but the post was far from being a permanent position. Duff Cooper held the post at the onset of war, but Chamberlain decided he had to go and replaced him with Leslie Hore-Belisha (the namesake of the flashing Belisha beacons common around the country), only to replace him soon after with Oliver Stanley. Chamberlain's departure from Downing Street was accompanied by Stanley's departure from the War Office, as Churchill replaced him with Anthony Eden. Eden was soon to move back to the Foreign Office, being replaced by David Margesson. Margesson's tenure was significantly longer, lasting until 1942, when Singapore fell, after which he was replaced by Sir Percy Grigg, who saw out the end of the war.

The War Office foundations had been strengthened in the 1930s in preparation for a possible war. In the event, the building was hit by German

The imposing Old War Office Building on Whitehall that was never quite big enough.

bombs several times. On 8 October 1940, a bomb killed one person and caused some superficial damage. Seven other bombs were to hit the building during the war, damaging some of the upper levels. During these raids staff could go to the relative safety of the sub-basement, where there was also an all-night canteen.

The War Office was a mix of many departments, all responsible for running their own parts of the military. Room 900, for example, was home to Intelligence School No. 9, or I.S.9(d), which was part of MI9, the escape and evasion organisation. While the majority of MI9 was to be found in Beaconsfield, once they had moved from the Metropole Building, I.S.9(d) and its secretive work remained in the War Office building.

I.S.9(d) was responsible for creating and maintaining escape lines – the organised routes through occupied territories along which Allied servicemen on the wrong side of the front line could be passed back to safety. I.S.9(d) sent agents and radio operators in to run these escape lines and developed protocols to improve security, especially once it was known that the Gestapo were making determined efforts to infiltrate them.

Being continually surrounded by Allied airmen and soldiers, the agents who ran the escape lines considerably increased their risk of discovery by infiltration or betrayal. But their work was vital in raising the morale of airmen who knew that if they bailed out over occupied territory there was an organisation that was capable of getting them home. The value of the successful return of thousands of men back to their own side to resume the fight cannot be underestimated.

The War Office continued to be the Army's administrative centre until 1964, when it was amalgamated with the Admiralty to form the Ministry of Defence. The building, which was from then on referred to as the Old War Office, was put up for sale by the MoD in 2013.

MoD Main Building
HORSE GUARDS AVENUE

Tube: Embankment
Barclays Cycle Hire: Embankment (Horse Guards), Westminster

The MoD main building is enclosed by Whitehall, the Victoria Embankment and Richmond Terrace, with its main entrance on HORSE GUARDS AVENUE.

To make way for the New Government Office building, which was primarily intended for the Board of Trade, buildings in Whitehall Gardens on the east side of Whitehall were demolished in 1938, after delays caused by the First World War and the Great Depression.

This work revealed the foundations of the Palace of Whitehall, and King Henry VIII's wine cellar. Queen Mary Steps from Whitehall Palace are still visible on the Thames side of the building, while the wine cellar was moved and incorporated into the new building.

Although two bombproof citadels were finished on the site by 1942, all other major building works ceased until the conclusion of the war.

The original intended occupants, the Board of Trade, moved into the north part of the building in 1951 while the Air Ministry moved into the remainder of the building in 1958. The whole building was handed over to the new Ministry of Defence which had been created by the merger of the three service ministries in 1964. Around 2003 the building underwent a full refurbishment and has since been reoccupied by the MoD.

10 Downing Street
WHITEHALL

Tube: Westminster
Barclays Cycle Hire: Embankment (Horse Guards), Westminster

DOWNING STREET was completed in 1686, two years after the death of Sir George Downing, who commissioned the houses in the street that bears his name. The street has undergone many changes since then, but it was around 1732 that Number 10 was given to Walpole, Britain's first prime minister, by King George II. The house was accepted as the official residence of the first lord, the position now known as the prime minister. Later, No. 11 became the residence of the chancellor of the exchequer, while Nos 9 and 12 house staff associated with running those offices.

Once war was declared with Germany and the initial phoney war phase was entered, the need for Prime Minister Neville Chamberlain and his Cabinet to leave Downing Street did not arise. With no air raids over London, the government machine was able to operate with comparative normality from the offices it had always occupied.

Churchill took over the premiership in the heat of battle as the Wehrmacht forged its way across Europe, forcing the capitulation of the Belgian and Dutch armies, destroying the French Army and routing the British at Dunkirk. Initially Churchill remained at Admiralty House, dictating memos from his bed there, before moving into Number 10 later in the day. Churchill's preference was to carry out all his day-to-day work at Downing Street and was, by all accounts, resistant to the idea of leaving. However, from 7 September 1940 the Luftwaffe's attention turned to London, forcing Churchill and his cabinet to move.

The Downing Street buildings were old and vulnerable; even a near miss had the potential to flatten the building. At the time of the Munich Crisis, when war seemed imminent, preparations were made for the impending air assault on London. Part of these measures included constructing shelters for

The back of Downing Street; it was lucky to survive a near miss during a bombing raid in 1940.

the occupants of Nos 10 and 11, while other rooms on the garden level had additional wooden props inserted to support the roof should the building collapse. These arrangements addressed the immediate problem of survival, but did not allow for the fact that the government would need to operate even during air raids. As the Blitz intensified, the Cabinet carried out its work at the New Public Offices, on the corner of Great George Street and Storey's Gate, or the 'No. 10 Annex', as it was known.

Events on 14 October 1940 were to reinforce the need for Churchill and his Cabinet to move. Churchill later recalled having dinner in the garden room of Number 10 as the evening air raid began, and hearing the bombs falling, the closest landing in Horse Guards Parade. Churchill, by his own account, got up and ordered the cooks to the shelter away from the large kitchen window. A few minutes later a bomb landed close by causing much damage to the building, including the kitchen, fortuitously relieved of its staff. The bomb had fallen on the Treasury shelter 50 yards away, burying all under the rubble and killing three civil servant home guards. Looking back now, it seems unlikely Churchill would have survived had that bomb hit Number 10. In typical Churchill fashion and undeterred by events, he and his dinner guest put on their tin hats and watched the rest of the raid from the top of the Annex.

Churchill continued to use Number 10 for some of the day-to-day business of government after the Blitz had finished and described the initial period after 7 September, before moving to the Annex, as 'exciting' and that 'one might as well have been at a battalion headquarters in the line'.

Downing Street is still home to the British prime minister and remains much as it did in the 1940s, only with much additional security preventing any public access along the street.

Foreign and Commonwealth Office
KING CHARLES STREET

Tube: Westminster
Barclays Cycle Hire: Embankment (Horse Guards), Westminster

The Foreign Office on KING CHARLES STREET, designed by George Gilbert Scott, was completed in 1868.

The Foreign Office was, and still is, responsible for the operation of the Secret Intelligence Service. During the war, this meant that the Foreign Office had direct responsibility for the work of Bletchley Park, who were sending, on average, 1,000 decrypted reports a month to the King Charles Street office.

The building is still used by the Foreign Office today, although it was nearly demolished in the 1960s. A restoration programme, started in the 1980s, returned the building to its original splendour and it is now a Grade I listed building.

The resplendent Foreign and Commonwealth Office, whose mandarins oversaw the wartime activities of the Secret Intelligence Service.

Cabinet War Rooms and No. 10 Annex
HM TREASURY, 1 HORSE GUARDS ROAD, CLIVE STEPS

Tube: Westminster
Barclays Cycle Hire: Embankment (Horse Guards), Westminster

The entrance to the Cabinet War Rooms can be found at the back of the Treasury, on the St James's Park side, by Clive Steps on the junction of HORSE GUARDS ROAD and King Charles Street.

The New Public Offices (NPO), as they were originally known, were completed in 1917 and occupied by several different government departments until the Treasury moved in during 1940.

There had been a concern, ever since the Zeppelin raids over Britain during the First World War, that London would be the target of aerial bombardment during any future conflict. With the spectre of war looming, the decision was made in 1938 to convert the basement of a Whitehall building into a protective shelter, covering a huge area, with every conceivable facility, to ensure that the government machine could continue to operate during any such attack.

The Office of Works decided that the basement of the NPO building on the corner of Great George Street and Storey's Gate was the most suited to the task, and work began on the conversion during 1938. The rooms were opened in August 1939, with the king paying a visit on 30 August, just a few days before war was declared.

In the event, the devastating air raids did not materialise immediately as feared. As a result Chamberlain only ever used the Cabinet War Rooms on one occasion, in October 1939. Despite the lack of ministerial use, the War Rooms were constantly utilised, with the Map Room being manned twenty-four hours a day. The demand for space in the War Rooms led to severe overcrowding problems that prompted the decision to expand them, both horizontally and vertically, until, by 1941, they were three times their original size. The Slab was a protective 3m-thick layer of reinforced concrete built above the War Rooms that also had to be extended. It stretched beyond the perimeter of the actual NPO building, covering adjacent courtyards.

A concrete apron, intended to strengthen the building, was also placed on the western side of the building, facing St James's Park. This incongruous feature can still be seen at the base of the building. A final safety feature was the large torpedo net slung across the western courtyard in the hope that it would catch any bombs heading for the main part of the building.

The NPO building was gradually taken over by departments essential to the running of the war and became known as the No. 10 Annex. This is where Churchill spent much of his time after being forced out of Number 10 proper. While the NPO was being prepared, the disused Underground station

The New Public Offices building, with the concrete apron that was added to help protect the War Rooms below.

at Down Street was used by the prime minister and the Cabinet on several occasions (see Down Street, p. 169).

There was, however, one issue (and a significant one) in that it was not believed that the Annex or the War Rooms, even with their protective slab, could withstand a direct hit, comprising as they did of converted basements rather than being purpose built. To address this issue, and to create a last command post in case of German invasion, a secondary complex, referred to as Paddock, was built at the Post Office Research and Development Station in Dollis Hill.

Returning to the War Rooms now gives a fascinating insight into the past. After the cessation of hostilities with Japan, the rooms were locked and mothballed for three years, at which point Parliament decided that they were a historic site that should be preserved. However, they were to remain virtually untouched for nearly three further decades, with access being limited during that time and their existence still only known to a small number of people. It was not until the late 1970s that the Imperial War Museum began their restoration work, with the first parts opening in 1984. Finally, in 2003 the entire complex was revealed to the public, almost sixty years after they were vacated by Churchill and his staff.

HM Treasury still occupies the Government Offices Great George Street, as they have done since 1940.

The Rotundas
MONCK STREET

Tube: St James's Park
Barclays Cycle Hire: Horseferry Road, Westminster

As the threat of war increased, so did the need for centrally located bombproof structures where government departments could work in safety.

One of the largest was on MONCK STREET, which is off Great Peter Street, west of Westminster Abbey. Two large gasholders, which had been demolished, had left deep circular holes where they had stood. These holes were used as the foundations of two great circular concrete rotundas, with one level below ground and four above.

Like the Admiralty Citadel on Horse Guards Parade, these structures were built to fulfil a very practical and urgent need. But, unlike the more obvious citadel on Horse Guards Parade, the Rotunda on Monck Street was demolished around 2001 to be replaced by offices and apartments.

New Scotland Yard
THE NORMAN SHAW BUILDINGS, VICTORIA EMBANKMENT

Tube: Westminster
Barclays Cycle Hire: Embankment (Horse Guards), Westminster

The headquarters of the Metropolitan Police Service (the Met) from 1890 to 1967 were at New Scotland Yard. The magnificent Norman Shaw Buildings, which were purpose built for the Met, can be found on the VICTORIA EMBANKMENT next to Westminster Bridge,

The Met's responsibilities in war were, as ever, to maintain law and order, but they also had additional duties such as enforcing the blackout and assisting with evacuations. The Emergency Powers (Defence) Act 1939 came into force on 24 August 1939, just before war was declared, and gave the authorities powers to make regulations that 'appeared' necessary to secure

The Norman Shaw Buildings, named after the architect who designed them and home to the Metropolitan Police throughout the war.

'public safety' and 'the defence of the realm'. This act, in reality, resulted in a greatly increased workload for the Met, with over 2,000 such Acts of Parliament being passed in the first year of war alone.

The police service was believed to be undermanned by 3 per cent, so as extra wartime duties stretched the police service, more manpower had to be brought in. One of the greatest increases was not achieved with men at all, but women, with the creation of the Women's Auxiliary Police Corps (WAPC). WAPC members started filling clerical and chauffeuring jobs, but the corps was soon performing more varied duties. The WAPC eventually peaked at 3,700 members in 1945. After it was disbanded at the end of the war many women from the WAPC joined the police service as regular officers.

The Met were to remain in the Norman Shaw Buildings until their move to new headquarters at 10 Broadway in 1967. The buildings, now called the Norman Shaw Buildings after the architect who designed them, are used as parliamentary offices.

Church House
DEAN'S YARD

Tube: Westminster
Barclays Cycle Hire: Embankment (Horse Guards), Westminster

CHURCH HOUSE can be found just off Broad Sanctuary behind Westminster Abbey and was used as the temporary debating chambers for the houses of lords and commons during the war (see Palace of Westminster, p. 110).

Church House is now a conference centre and venue for product launches, dinners and award ceremonies. Do not be deterred by the barrier near the entrance to Westminster Abbey (there is also a small gateway at the back); it is quite acceptable to go into Dean's Yard which offers a surprisingly tranquil setting right next to Parliament Square.

Church House, which was opened by the king and queen on 10 June 1940 and was to be used by both Houses during the war.

Palace of Westminster
PARLIAMENT SQUARE

Tube: Westminster
Barclays Cycle Hire: Embankment (Horse Guards), Westminster

The Palace of Westminster, which is home to the House of Lords, the House of Commons, the Elizabeth Tower and Big Ben, can be found on the banks of the River Thames. A group of conspirators, including Guido Fawkes, famously tried to blow them up in 1605; where they failed, the Luftwaffe nearly succeeded.

The House of Commons is where Members of Parliament have gathered for centuries to debate policy and govern the country. It was here that Chamberlain's political career ended after a debate in May 1940, when Leo Amery MP, quoting Oliver Cromwell, famously declared: 'You have sat here too long for any good you are doing. Depart, I say, and let us have done with you. In the name of God, go!'

The vulnerability of the Westminster Palace was appreciated, with Churchill asking for 'alternative accommodation to be found'. Assembling the entire leadership of the country in one location was an enormous risk, even when the daylight bombing raids ceased, since debates could continue long into the night. In one memo Churchill stated: 'it is only a question of time before these buildings and chambers are struck. We must hope they will be stuck when not occupied by their Members.'

It was not long before the building was damaged by the first of fourteen bombs that hit it during the war. One destroyed the south window of Westminster Hall in September 1940, with another devastating the south and east side of Cloisters in December 1940. The House of Commons Chamber, from where Churchill gave some of his finest speeches, was to be turned to rubble on the nights of 10 and 11 May 1941 when an incendiary bomb crashed through the roof. Not being able to save both Westminster Hall and the Commons Chamber, the fire service concentrated on the hall; by the next day the Commons Chamber was a smouldering shell.

While no one was hurt, the chamber was ruined and the business of parliament had to be carried out in the Lords Chamber, while the Lords met in the Robing Room, or at Church House behind Westminster Abbey. It was not until 1950 that work to rebuild the Commons Chamber was completed, but the archway through which you enter the House of Commons was not repaired, to remind MPs of that terrible night.

The House of Commons is now open to the public and it is possible to go on a guided tour of the building on Saturdays and during the summer.

Westminster Abbey

PARLIAMENT SQUARE

Tube: Westminster
Barclays Cycle Hire: Embankment (Horse Guards), Westminster

Westminster Abbey overlooks PARLIAMENT SQUARE and has been used for state occasions since 1066, such as royal weddings (including George VI's marriage to Elizabeth in 1923), funerals (it is the resting place of seventeen monarchs) and state coronations.

At the outbreak of war, anything of value was removed from the abbey. Some artefacts, such as the medieval tombs, which could not be moved, were protected using around 60,000 sandbags.

Westminster Abbey was bombed and badly damaged but remained standing throughout the war.

In the early hours of 11 May 1941 the abbey roof was set ablaze by an incendiary bomb lodged in the rafters that could not be extinguished. Much damage was done to the main part of the abbey, not just by the fire but by the water used to extinguish the blaze. Other buildings that were part of the abbey, such as the Deanery, Cheyneygates and Westminster School Hall, were all destroyed.

On VE day short memorial services were held at the abbey and were attended by an estimated 25,000 people. The abbey is open to the public all week except Sundays.

Big Ben is seen through barbed wire, which had been placed at strategic points as defence against a possible German invasion.

The area of London from Regent's Park to Hackney, north of the Euston Road in the east and Hackney Road in the west, covers a vast swathe of northern London. It has within it the mainline stations of Euston, King's Cross and St Pancras, now St Pancras International, home to the Eurostar train service to France.

The whole area suffered much bombing during the war, but was sufficiently distant from the main targets of central London that it avoided the same concentrated bombing experienced by the Docklands and the City.

One of the most enthralling tales of the war was that of Operation Mincemeat, and the parts played by St Pancras and Hackney coroner's offices in the journey of Glyndwr Michael who, after his death, was to be the key to one of the biggest and most ingenious wartime deceptions.

Central Hackney following bombing on 19–20 March 1941.

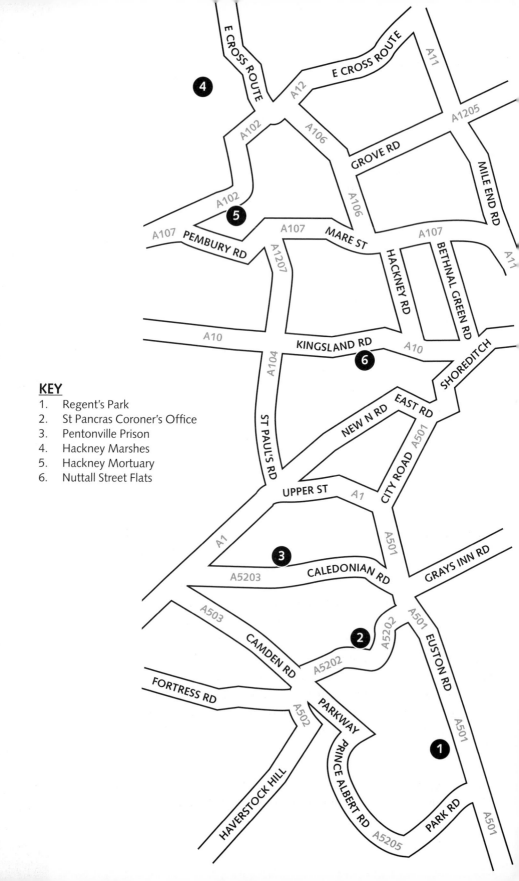

KEY

1. Regent's Park
2. St Pancras Coroner's Office
3. Pentonville Prison
4. Hackney Marshes
5. Hackney Mortuary
6. Nuttall Street Flats

Regent's Park

Tube: Regent's Park
Barclays Cycle Hire: The Tennis Courts, Regent's Park

REGENT'S PARK is one of the large royal parks to be found in London. Its southern side lies just north of Marylebone Road and stretches all the way up to London Zoo, covering an area of 395 acres. It opened to the public in 1835.

During the war many of the parks in London had anti-aircraft (AA) batteries located in them, with the large open spaces being ideal sites. AA Command was formed in 1939 and was to be commanded by General Frederick Pile for the duration of the war. At its founding, AA Command was considerably under strength, but the lull of the phoney war allowed some time for extra guns and ammunition to be constructed and distributed. As 1940 wore on, the number of men and women in AA Command had swollen to half a million.

There were many complexities in the use of AA guns, most important of which were ensuring that they did not hit their own aircraft. This meant their use might be restricted at times. However, any perceived inactivity was criticised by some Londoners for whom the guns were a visible and audible sign that Britain was hitting back at the Luftwaffe raiders.

Barrage balloons, simply intended as aerial obstacles designed to get in the way of aircraft dive-bombing a target, were launched from the park as well as being used extensively around other important potential targets, from the docks to the Houses of Parliament.

The park was also used by bomb disposal teams who scoured London for the multitude of Luftwaffe ordnance that had failed to detonate. Once a bomb had safely been defused, or was deemed safe to move, it was taken to an area of open ground to be destroyed. Regent's Park was one place that was used for bomb disposal, with the Earl of Suffolk being a regular visitor. Having being denied a return to active service for health reasons, Lord Suffolk used his considerable connections to get a position working for the Ministry of Supply in France. As the German advance overwhelmed the country, Lord Suffolk made it his mission to extract as many French scientists as possible; however, they were not all he came back with. He was also to return with a large quantity of industrial-grade diamonds and several barrels of heavy water, as used in early atomic weapons research (see Norwegian Government in Exile, p. 115). Safely back in Britain, Lord Suffolk put his mind to bomb disposal. Regent's Park was one of several places he used to have bombs delivered to carry out research on. The earl was to meet an untimely end when a bomb he was working on in Erith Marshes in Kent detonated, killing him, his driver, his secretary and several soldiers instantly.

St Pancras Coroner's Office
CAMLEY STREET

Tube: Mornington Crescent
Barclays Cycle Hire: Royal College Street, Camden Town

St Pancras coroner's office and mortuary can still be found on CAMLEY STREET and backs on to St Pancras Hospital and St Pancras Gardens.

The invasion of mainland Europe was to start in the Mediterranean, code-named Operation Husky. Allied forces were to depart from North Africa and land on Sicily before invading Italy. Of the many problems facing the planners was the obviousness of this attack route, which would result in a massive reinforcement of Sicily by the Germans, making the landings a costly affair. So, the question posed was 'how to make the Germans think otherwise?'

It was the ingenious character of Charles Cholmondeley who came up with the idea of planting a host of fictitious documents about the body of a fake soldier with the hope of them falling into enemy hands as a modern-day Trojan horse.

At this stage the idea seemed relatively simple: acquire a cadaver, load it with documents that implied the next Allied attack would be in the directions of Greece and Sardinia, bypassing the real target of Sicily. Then feed the body, and thus the documents, to the Germans via Franco's Spain.

Ewen Montagu was to lead this deception, but immediately came upon the first problem: getting a suitable body that looked like the cause of death

St Pancras Coroner's Office, where the body of Glyndwr Michael came to the attention of the Operation Mincemeat team.

had been drowning. It was noted at the time that, although there were hundreds of bodies available, it being a war and all, they tended to die 'in the wrong way'.

Montagu put his old friend Bentley Purchase, the coroner at St Pancras coroner's office, on the lookout for a suitable body. The body of Glyndwr Michael, a man who had killed himself with rat poison, came to Purchase's attention and, after a swift inquest, the body was put in cold storage in St Pancras mortuary on or shortly after 28 January 1943, where he was to wait until he was needed around three months later when Operation Mincemeat was put into action (see Hackney Mortuary, p. 119).

Pentonville Prison
CALEDONIAN ROAD

Tube: Caledonian Road and Barnsbury
Barclays Cycle Hire: None close

Pentonville Prison is in the borough of Islington and is just north-west of the stations at King's Cross and St Pancras International. Opened in 1842, it was the prototype prison design of Major Jebb and still operates today with a capacity of around 1,200.

Even though the Blitz sprit generally prevailed, crime did not disappear overnight and looting of bombed-out homes and businesses meant the courts and prisons had a lively trade. Another crime that was fortunately less prevalent, but that the security forces were guarding against, was treachery. For various reasons men and women were prepared to betray their country and work for the Nazis despite the potential for it to end with the hangman's noose should they be caught.

Oswald Job's life ended in Pentonville Prison on 16 March 1944. Job had gone to France after the First World War where he had a successful business, but was interned by the Germans in 1940. He spent three years in St Denis internment camp where he worked as a translator for his captors. His story that he had escaped and made his way to Spain was soon proven to be false. Firstly, via a double agent, MI5 were aware that a man 'carrying jewellery to pay an agent would be entering the country' (*Letting the Side Down, British Traitors of The Second World War*, Murphy, 2006) hence diamonds in Job's possession caused immediate suspicion. Then, when Job's brother's house was raided, secret ink crystals were found in hollowed out keys and other materials in a safety razor. Oswald Job was tried and sentenced to death for attempting to spy for the Germans, although he maintained he had no intention of doing so and his acts were simply those of a desperate man trying to escape.

Another, more notorious man executed at Pentonville was one Theodore Schurch. Schurch's treachery dated back to the mid-1930s, when he joined Mosley's fascist movement. Mosley was a Member of Parliament and the founder of the British Union of Fascists who believed that Britain should follow in the footsteps of Nazi Germany.

Although only 17, Schurch was approached by a man who said he 'could do much more for the movement' and encouraged him to enter the British Army, even going so far as to instruct him to volunteer as a driver. This was to enable him to better observe, and then report on, Army movements to the Italian Intelligence Service.

Up to and throughout the war, Schurch gave valuable information about unit strengths and movements until he was captured at Tobruk, where he immediately asked to be put in contact with Italian Intelligence. Schurch was now to work directly for the Italians and Germans as a stool pigeon, infiltrating captured soldiers to gain what information he could before passing it on. He was even put in contact with captured SAS soldiers, including their founder, David Sterling, although there is no suggestion he handed over anything of use.

His final act was to masquerade as an escaped prisoner to try to infiltrate Italian resistance movements, but soon found himself captured by the rapidly advancing Americans ,who handed him over to the British as a 'potential political prisoner'. He confessed all his activities to the British authorities and was sent to Pentonville where he was executed on 4 January 1946.

Hackney Marshes

Tube: Hackney Wick
Barclays Cycle Hire: None close

HACKNEY MARSHES cover a massive area of land which has spurs of the River Lea either side of it and joins the northern end of the London 2012 Olympic site.

In the lead up to war councils were instructed to dig trenches, ostensibly for air-raid protection, though it seemed to many to be a rather limited gesture. However, many parks and other open spaces such as Hackney Marshes and Hackney Downs were soon being dug up as more and more trenches were constructed.

The Marshes were also used, as were many of London's large open spaces, to site the anti-aircraft batteries defending the capital against Luftwaffe raiders. As a result of these bombing raids on the city there were many unexploded bombs for the brave bomb disposal teams to defuse. Bombs needing to be disposed of would often be taken to the vast expanse of Hackney Marshes, where they could be detonated in safety; it is here that a bomb extracted from near the foundations of St Paul's Cathedral was destroyed.

Those bombs that did explode as intended were reducing parts of London to nothing more than rubble. As part of the clearing up process, this fallen brick and masonry was removed and dumped in Hackney Marshes.

Hackney Mortuary
ST JOHN'S CHURCHYARD, LOWER CLAPTON ROAD

Tube: Caledonian Hackney Central
Barclays Cycle Hire: None close

Hackney Mortuary can be found off LOWER CLAPTON ROAD in St John's churchyard, which is at the southern end of Clapton Square

Operation Mincemeat was the extraordinary plan to deceive the Germans about Allied plans to invade Italy, via Sicily, by planting a host of fictitious documents on a dead major, indicating that the axis of attack would be via Greece and Sardinia. When Operation Mincemeat was put into action (see St Pancras Coroner's Office, p. 116), the first stop in a long journey from St Pancras to Spain for 'Major Martin' was at Hackney Mortuary. It was here that undertaker Ivor Leverton was told to take the body at 1 a.m. on 17 April 1943.

Once at Hackney mortuary, Montagu, Cholmondeley, Purchase and the rest of the team set about adding the final clothing and all-important documents. The only problem they appear to have encountered was in getting his boots on, as the 'major's' feet had frozen solid, a problem solved by defrosting them using an electric heater. From Hackney mortuary, the body was driven up to Scotland and placed on board the submarine HMS *Seraph* for the remainder of the journey to Spanish waters.

Once the body was discovered, the papers being carried by 'Major Martin' detailing the fake landings aimed at Greece and Sardinia were duly handed over to the Germans, who copied them before allowing the body to be returned to the British. From Ultra intercepts it was seen that the fake plans were indeed turning heads in Germany's High Command, reaching all the way up to Dönitz, Jodl and even Hitler.

The overall deception plan – Operation Barclay – designed to hide Sicily as the real target was also running alongside Mincemeat. It seems that they were successful as, having met little resistance, more than 100,000 men were ashore on Sicily by the end of the first day and the conquest of the island had begun.

Nuttall Street Flats
NUTTALL STREET

Tube: Haggerston
Barclays Cycle Hire: None close

NUTTALL STREET is off the Kingsland Road, which runs north from the junction of Shoreditch High Street and Hackney Road.

On the night of 29 September 1940, the council flats on Nuttall Street were hit by a bomb, causing extensive damage and killing many people, including thirteen from a single family. The explosion was so extensive that some of the nurses' homes in nearby St Leonard's Hospital also had to be demolished.

Air-raid Precaution Northern Report Centre
24 ROSSENDALE STREET

Train: Clapton
Barclays Cycle Hire: None close

One of the most fascinating buildings to survive from the war was the Air-raid Precaution (ARP) Northern Report Centre. Air-raid precaution schemes were initiated in July 1935, four years before the German invasion of Poland that finally brought Britain into conflict with Nazi Germany. How well ARPs were put into place differed from council to council within London's boroughs. However, the Air Raid Precautions and Civil Defence Acts passed in 1937 and 1939 ended any choice councils may have been able to exercise as to the extent they were implementing ARPs.

Hackney was certainly making progress, and by 1938 had a command system in place with the basement of Hackney Town Hall as its centre, and which the ARP Northern Report Centre on Rossendale Street was part of. This system allowed the ARP officers to co-ordinate their resources such as fire fighters and rescuers as well as repair work teams in the aftermath of bombing raids.

Opened in 1938 at 24 Rossendale Street, Clapton, the centre is partially sunk into the ground and accessed by steps that descend down into the main room via an airlock door system, installed in case of a gas attack. The main area was subdivided into four separate rooms including a plant room, toilet, a main room and control room.

The building was used by the Civil Defence Corps until they were disbanded in 1968. It is quite amazing that the building has not only survived, but so have many of its contents, such as a gas mask, stretcher, siren, bikes and plant material. The building, while being preserved, has been built over by apartments in recent years and is no longer visible from the street.

The area covered in this chapter starts at the busy Piccadilly Circus and borders Whitehall along Northumberland Avenue, going as far as Farringdon Road in the east. While it does not have the tightly packed buildings of Whitehall or Marylebone, there is much to discover.

Piccadilly was the centre of London nightlife, from the Ritz, one of London's most famous hotels and refuge of the rich and dispossessed of Europe, to Piccadilly Circus, a hub of wartime entertainment. The Circus was frequented by soldiers on leave, young women and later the American GIs that flooded the country in the build-up to D-Day. However, with the blackout, it lost much of its pre- and post-war impact as the famous lights were doused for the duration of the conflict. The introduction of an American Red Cross service club on Piccadilly, known as 'Rainbow Corner', brightened things up. Open twenty-four hours a day, service clubs allowed American soldiers to buy home comforts otherwise unobtainable in Britain, such as an all-essential doughnut.

Moving on towards Leicester Square is theatre land, where the Café de Paris, scene of a terrible bombing incident, and the Windmill Club, famous in equal measure for its nude shows and for staying open for the duration of the war, can both be found.

From here on, more official buildings can be found, such as the hotels converted to offices on Northumberland Avenue and the Canadian Air Force Headquarters at Lincoln's Inn Fields. In between all of this there are the wartime homes of some of the period's most interesting characters.

Today, Piccadilly is still very much an area of clubs, bars and theatres, while offices take up much of the Aldwych end.

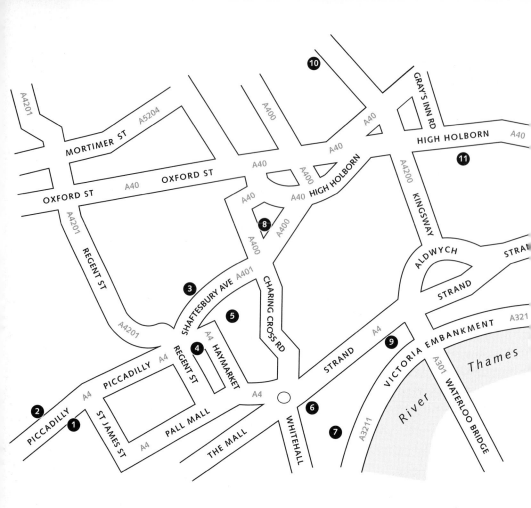

KEY

1. The Ritz Hotel
2. Dutch Government in Exile
3. The Windmill Club
4. Eros Statue
5. Café de Paris
6. The Victoria Hotel
7. The Metropole Hotel
8. Leo Marks's Wartime Residence
9. The Savoy Hotel
10. Forest 'the White Rabbit' Yeo-Thomas's Wartime Residence (just off map)
11. Royal Canadian Air Force Headquarters

The Ritz Hotel
150 PICCADILLY

Tube: Green Park
Barclays Cycle Hire: Green Park Station, West End

The Ritz Hotel London can be found a few hundred yards down from Piccadilly Circus, next to Green Park. Construction on the steel-framed hotel began in 1905, and it opened its doors in 1906, quickly establishing itself as one of London's premier hotels. The Ritz, along with the other grand London hotels, vied for the trade of the capital's most affluent citizens. However, the Ritz was able to advertise that its steel structure improved its strength, and hence safety, to attract guests. While possibly not as successful as the Savoy or Dorchester, the Ritz certainly stood out in London society at the time. Summit meetings were held in the Marie Antoinette Suite, a private dining room, by Eisenhower, de Gaulle and Churchill in the build-up to the cross-Channel invasion.

If not their most distinguished guest, one of the most interesting was King Zog of Albania, who had been elected president in 1925 and elevated to king in 1928. When, on Good Friday 1939, Albania's strategic ally, Italy, invaded, there was little the country's ill-equipped armed forces could do to resist.

Refuge to royalty and the location of meetings between Churchill, de Gaulle and Eisenhower, the Ritz lasted out the war in style.

Within a matter of days the country had become an annex of Italy, and King Zog, his family and entourage had fled to London to take up residence on the third floor of the Ritz. Like many other banished leaders of that period, Zog did not return to the country he had ruled prior to the war and lived out his life in exile.

The Ritz is as iconic today as it was during the war and is as opulent as ever, with a £50 million refurbishment having taken place in the mid-nineties.

Dutch Government in Exile
STRATTON HOUSE, PICCADILLY

Tube: Green Park
Barclays Cycle Hire: Green Park Station, West End

Stratton House can be found on the corner of PICCADILLY and Stratton Street, and is opposite the Ritz and Green Park.

The Netherlands, like many of Europe's nations, was not prepared for war, and especially war on the scale envisaged by Hitler and the Nazis. Its relatively small population simply did not lend itself to a large standing army capable of repelling the Nazi war machine.

Diplomatically, the Netherlands found itself in an awkward position. With no hope of protection by the British and French armies massing on the Belgium border until such time as they might repel any advance through Flanders, the Dutch took the only realistic option open to them and declared neutrality. The simple hope was that they would be bypassed by any German advance and spared the devastation of invasion, something they felt inevitable had they openly sided with Britain and France. Their neutral status was to be flagrantly violated and the country invaded as German troops crossed their borders, as well as those of Luxembourg and Belgium, on 10 May 1940. The Dutch Army fought a tenacious and gallant, if short-lived, defence of their country, finally laying down their arms after five days to save further bloodshed and destruction. Strategically, the decision to cease open resistance little influenced the Battle of France that was about to unfold to the south and was seen as a necessary step by the Dutch government and royal family to save the country.

Unlike the Belgian King Leopold a few months later, the Dutch refused to surrender out of hand to the Germans, preferring to continue the fight in exile until such time as they regained their homeland. Queen Wilhelmina and her Cabinet moved to London, leaving the Netherlands on board a Royal Navy ship shortly after the invasion. They arrived in London and moved into Stratton House, opposite Green Park Underground station, where they remained running their government in exile for the duration of the war.

The Dutch, while not great in number, constructively added to the Allied war effort throughout the period of conflict. Queen Wilhelmina regularly broadcast to Dutch citizens via Radio Oranje, particularly encouraging those suffering under Nazi occupation to be strong and to resist. This was a call taken up by many, and the resistance movement was very strong within the Netherlands, with SOE sending many agents over there throughout the war.

The Allied campaign through mainland Europe entered the Netherlands in dramatic fashion in the form of Operation Market Garden, the brave but ill-fated mission to jump the Rhine, conceived by Montgomery. This operation failed in its principal objective, but the Netherlands were liberated nonetheless and Queen Wilhelmina returned to her beloved homeland on 2 May 1945.

The Windmill Club
17–19 GREAT WINDMILL STREET

Tube: Piccadilly Circus
Barclays Cycle Hire: Wardour Street, Soho

Laura Henderson brought a small theatre in GREAT WINDMILL STREET, which opened in 1931 as the Windmill. Its early days did not meet with great success and it was not until the manager, Vivian van Damm, put on the first nude shows in London, allowed only if the models did not move, that the theatre really took off.

The Windmill was famous for being the club that never closed, remaining open continuously for the duration of the war, except for twelve days from 4 September to 16 September 1939, when all theatres were forced to close by the authorities. During the worst bombing of the Blitz, patrons and performers were able to use the basement as an air-raid shelter, from where they emerged to carry on with the show. Around 1943 the theatre coined its famous phrase 'we never closed!', although this was soon to be altered by the public to 'we never clothed!'

The Windmill was forever enshrined in Second Word War legend when *Life Magazine* ran a feature on the club. The magazine described the day-to-day life of the performers and their routines that carried on, unabated, during the worst of Blitz. Performers and stagehands would spend the night at the theatre when unable to get home simply because it was too dangerous, something that the Windmill girls were even able to make look glamorous, reclining in their dressing rooms with tin hats at the ready.

The Windmill girls and other staff at the theatre did not confine themselves to the theatre. They took their shows on the road, performing at aircraft hangars and drill halls across the country to entertain the troops.

During nights in London they also did their stint fire watching from the roof of the building.

The Windmill continued to run after the war and was to see Peter Sellers, Harry Seacombe, Tony Hancock and Bruce Forsyth all start their careers there, while a film starring Judi Dench and Bob Hoskins called *Mrs Henderson Presents* was also made about the club in 2005. The club now opens under the name The Windmill International as a table-dancing nightclub and is very much for adults only.

Eros Statue
PICCADILLY

Tube: Piccadilly Circus
Barclays Cycle Hire: Panton Street, West End

The statue of Eros was originally located in the roundabout that was in the centre of the Piccadilly Road junction. It has since been moved a short distance to accommodate changes in the layout, but is still very close to the Piccadilly Underground station entrance.

Built in 1893 to commemorate the philanthropist Lord Shaftsbury, the statue was topped by Eros, who is made out of aluminium. The statue, along with many others such as that of King Charles I in front of Trafalgar Square, was covered up for protection; it was surrounded by sandbags and then encased in wood. Eros, along with London's other statues, was to remain entombed until the end of the war.

Eros at Piccadilly, entombed with sandbags and wood for protection during the war.

Café de Paris
3–4 COVENTRY STREET

Tube: Piccadilly Circus
Barclays Cycle Hire: Panton Street, West End

The Café de Paris, which opened in 1924, can be found in the busy Piccadilly area of London in COVENTRY STREET, a short distance from Piccadilly Underground station. After an impromptu visit, the Prince of Wales became a regular visitor and business was soon booming as the Café de Paris became one of 'the' venues to be seen at in the 1920s and 1930s.

The Café de Paris remained a popular club, restaurant and dance venue during the Blitz, with live bands playing into the night. This was in part because maître d' Martin Poulson advertised the venue as being safe from the bombs above. From the street-level entrance you descend down into the basement club, which would have given the illusion of safety; in most situations it would have been. However, disaster was to strike on the night of 8 March 1941.

Ken 'Snakehips' Johnson and his band were playing at the club and the dance floor was crowded with revellers. Two bombs struck the club, possibly hitting a ventilation shaft that allowed them to travel directly into the heart of the club. One detonated above the band while the other exploded on the dance floor. Snakehips and all but one of his band, Leslie 'Jiver' Hutchinson, were instantly killed, just some of the eighty people in total that died that night. The casualties were especially high, but would have been higher if the bombs had struck an hour later as the club would have been reaching its capacity. The injuries were horrific due to the enclosed space that the bombs exploded in. There were reports of scattered limbs and headless bodies, as well as people sat without a mark on them, dead. This was put down to the suddenness of the explosion sucking the air out of the room, causing their lungs to explode.

The devastation at the Café de Paris was not just met by rescuers, but also by looters, revealing a darker side of some Londoners during the Blitz. In amongst the confusion of rubble, the injured and rescue workers, looters slipped in with ease, taking wallets and necklaces from the dead, some even resorted to cutting off a finger to get a ring.

The bomb that destroyed the Café de Paris was extraordinary in its accuracy, but the incident again highlighted that nowhere was truly safe from the 'lucky bomb' that was a direct hit.

The Café de Paris was back in business after the war, reopening after a £7,500 refurbishment in 1948. It is still open today as one of London's most opulent venues for cabaret, club nights, live music, special events and weddings.

The Victoria Hotel

8 NORTHUMBERLAND AVENUE

Tube: Charing Cross
Barclays Cycle Hire: Northumberland Avenue, Strand

The Victoria Hotel, just off Trafalgar Square at 8 NORTHUMBERLAND AVENUE, opened in 1887 at a cost of £520,000 and at the time was one of the biggest hotels in London with 500 rooms.

It closed in 1940 when the hotel was requisitioned by the War Office, along with many other hotels in the area, and occupied by the Quartermaster General's Directorate.

Room 238 had much more interesting goings-on, however, soon being put to good use by SOE. SOE did not have the luxury of time to develop as an organisation and was in desperate need of new recruits. Unable to advertise directly, they used a variety of methods to talent-spot potential recruits, with a first requirement being fluency in a foreign language.

Potential recruits were then invited to go for an interview to determine whether they were made of the 'right stuff' for SOE work. Many of these interviews were carried out by Selwyn Jepson in Room 238 of the Victoria Hotel, although he also used offices at Sanctuary Building, part of the Ministry of Pensions, for the same purpose.

Jepson was an author of books such as *I Met Murder*, *A Noise in the Night* and *Man Running*, on which the Hitchcock film *Stage Fright* was based. Jepson's role was to talk to the potential agents and try to determine whether or not they would be up to the tasks that SOE would be asking them to carry out: to go into enemy-occupied territory and operate as an agent there. The extreme danger could not be underestimated, but it was not simply a case of being captured and made a prisoner of war; it was a case of being captured by the Gestapo, tortured and quite likely executed, all fates met by many SOE agents. Jepson, in a relatively short time, had to try to decide if they would be up to those challenges, and although the candidate would have time to consider all this information before giving an answer, ultimately it was Jepson who had the final say.

During the course of the war he interviewed notable agents such as Violette Szabo, who was to die in Ravensbrück concentration camp. Another agent he interviewed was Noor Inayat Khan. Khan had an Indian father and American mother and was brought up in France. After intensive SOE training, Khan flew into France by Lysander on 16 June 1943, but was arrested by the Gestapo in October of the same year. Gradually the various circuits operating in Paris had been infiltrated by the Gestapo and Khan was left as the only wireless operator. Despite clear indications that the Gestapo were getting closer, and instructions from London to come back, Khan refused and stayed on. The biggest disaster, however, was to follow: the Gestapo were able to continue to operate her wireless set, thus duping London into thinking that Khan was still safe. This resulted in agents being dropped into France straight into enemy hands. Khan was eventually taken to Pforzheim concentration camp, and then on to Dachau where she was shot. For her bravery while serving with SOE in France, Khan was posthumously awarded the *Croix de Guerre* with gold star and later the George Cross.

Room 238 was later used by Vera Atkins, Buckmaster's personal assistant, to co-ordinate her search for SOE agents after the war had finished and to interview relatives of those agents to try to give them some idea of what had happened to their loved ones. It was Atkins who painstakingly pieced together the last moments in the lives of many SOE agents who died at the hands of the Nazis.

The Victoria Hotel did not reopen after the war and was purchased by the government in 1951. It was used as government and other offices before being left unoccupied for a number of years. It was eventually purchased by the London School of Economics, which opened it as a hall of residence in 2006.

The Metropole Hotel
CORINTHIA HOTEL LONDON, WHITEHALL PLACE

Tube: Charing Cross
Barclays Cycle Hire: Whitehall Place, Strand

The Metropole Hotel was built in 1883 for Fredrick Gordon and opened in 1885. The hotel was used by the War Office first during the First World War, opening again during the interwar years, but was again leased by the government in 1936 for £300,000.

It was to be used as temporary accommodation for departments moved from Whitehall Gardens, where the new government offices were to be built; these offices are now known as the MoD main building. However, the Metropole continued to be used throughout the war as an extension of the War Office, whose ranks continued to swell as the war gathered pace.

The escape and evasion organisation, MI9, also had its early roots in the Metropole Building, and its origins stemmed from the work of two men. The first was Captain A.R. Rawlinson, who was tasked with remobilising MI1a, the escape and evasion department created in the First World War. The second man was J.C.F. Holland, who was given a typist and told to research any subject he chose. This department was to become the Military Research Unit (MI(R)), and eventually became one of the original components of the

The Corinthia Hotel, known as the Metropole Building, was the first home of the escape and evasion organisation, MI9.

Special Operations Executive. The Joint Intelligence Committee (JIC) were keen on the development of a dedicated organisation and Holland put forward a list of candidates who he believed could lead it, with Norman Crockatt being chosen, an officer of the Great War complete with DSO and MC. Rawlinson was initially unaware that his fledgling MI1a department was to be replaced with something completely new, but was eagerly taken on board by Crockatt under his immediate command, where he remained for the rest of the war.

MI9 was officially created in a minute dated 23 December 1939, with their first office being Room 424 of the Metropole Hotel. MI9 started its work and was responsible for both British escapers and Axis prisoners, with the latter being under Rawlinson's command.

MI9 was an amazing organisation that was responsible for creating and developing escape lines to bring back downed airmen through occupied countries. The people who ran these lines were often ordinary civilians who put themselves in the utmost danger as they ran a constant risk from being in the company of clearly non-native airmen.

The organisation also put a great deal of effort into developing the means by which captured servicemen could escape. They soon developed training courses and lectured men on escape and evasion, although this was met with some resistance early on. By 1940, under the care of Clayton Hutton, MI9 had developed and were distributing special escape and evasion kits that were designed to keep a man going for forty-eight hours. They contained, amongst other things, malted milk tablets, matches, a compass, water-purifying tablets and a water bottle.

They then went on to develop escape tools such as concealed hacksaws and compasses disguised as buttons. They even arranged for all razor blades sold through forces canteens to be magnetised. Other items were sent to POWs hidden in parcels from relatives, such as blankets with the pattern of an overcoat that showed up when washed, which could be cut out and stitched into a civilian coat.

MI9 eventually outgrew Room 424, while Crockatt was finding the crowded Whitehall unsuitable for such clandestine work. A bomb that hit the Metropole Building in September 1940 was the final straw that persuaded him that a move was necessary, primarily because the damage and confusion caused by the resulting fire interfered with his work. MI9 moved three weeks later to Wilton Park in Beaconsfield.

The building continued to be used by various government departments after the war and, during the 1950s, contained a large number of personnel from the Air Ministry. It was used by the MoD until it was bought by the Corinthia Hotel Group in 2007, who transformed it back into a luxurious five-star hotel.

Leo Marks's Wartime Residence
84 CHARING CROSS ROAD

Tube: Leicester Square
Barclays Cycle Hire: Moor Street, Soho

No. 84 CHARING CROSS ROAD can be found just off Cambridge Circus, opposite the Palace Theatre, and was home to the famous bookshop Marks & Co. It was owned by Leo Marks's father and counted among its customers Field Marshal Alanbrooke, whose interest was in ornithology. The location of the shop is marked with a brass plaque.

Leo Marks's wartime career was remarkable, not only for his rapid rise through the Special Operations Executive, but also for his ingenious solutions to practical problems that were, in the bluntest terms, putting agents' lives in danger.

After being accepted to 'a school for cryptographers' in Bedford, he joined SOE on Baker Street. Here he described the rivalry he encountered between different factions and people intent on improving their rank, which was at times so bizarre as to be almost unbelievable.

No. 84 Charing Cross Road, location of the famous Marks & Co. bookshop and home to Leo Marks, SOE's coding genius.

From his first encounter with SOE, when he was asked to decode a message, Marks knew there was a problem with the coding system used and set about trying to change it. By the end of the war he had developed many new ideas and protocols to improve security and to deal with 'indecipherable' messages sent from the field (see p. 45).

Marks soon developed a deep sense of responsibility for 'his' agents, such as Violette Szabo, Noor Inayat Khan, Forest 'the White Rabbit' Yeo-Thomas and many others as he taught them the new coding methods they were to use before going on missions.

When SOE was disbanded, Marks went on to have a brief stint at MI6 before leaving to pursue other interests, most notably the writing of the film *Peeping Tom*. The bookshop itself became famous when Helene Hanff wrote a book about her correspondence with the shop's chief buyer, Frank Doel.

The Savoy Hotel
STRAND

Tube: Covent Garden
Barclays Cycle Hire: Southampton Street, Strand

The Savoy Hotel's entrance can be found on the STRAND, almost apologetically set back from the road, near Waterloo Bridge, and has views overlooking the Thames. Built by Richard d'Oyly Carte next to his Savoy Theatre, the hotel opened in 1889 and remained so throughout the war.

American journalists arriving in London looking for a hotel from where they could report on the Blitz, both in relative safety and comfort, looked no further than the Savoy. With their extravagant expense accounts, it became their favoured hangout, with the notable exception of Ed Murrow, who shunned this luxury to better experience the Blitz. The America Bar became so popular with the American journalists that Douglas Williams from the Ministry of Information moved the nightly briefings he gave to the Savoy.

The Savoy not only boasted deep basement shelters, but also had one of the best restaurants, the River Room, which is below street level on the Strand side but looks out across the Thames. The Savoy offered a haven to reporters, such as Whitelaw Reid, from war-torn London outside. Reid's family owned the influential paper the *Herald Tribune*, and he was learning the ropes of the family trade. Having just switched to reporting, Reid realised the biggest story of the century was unfolding in Britain – its likely downfall – and he wanted to be there. Reid's influence, via his family's position in the upper echelons of US society, afforded him lunch with Churchill and weekends away with the Edens. But when he was in London he stayed at the Savoy, even sleeping next to the queen's brother, David Bowes-Lyon, in the basement air-raid shelter, where mattresses were laid out. Nevertheless, Reid did upset the chef for commenting on his inventiveness with the ingredients to make the hors d'oeuvres.

The Savoy, like many of London's grand hotels, underwent complete refurbishment, beginning in 2007 and closed for the first time in 118 years. The hotel reopened in 2010, resplendent as ever.

Forest 'the White Rabbit' Yeo-Thomas's Wartime Residence
QUEEN COURT, GUILDFORD STREET

Tube: Russell Square
Barclays Cycle Hire: Guildford Street, Bloomsbury

Queen Court is a small block of flats on GUILDFORD STREET, which comes off Southampton Row directly opposite Russell Square and was home to SOE agent Forest Yeo-Thomas, also known as the 'White Rabbit' or 'Tommy'.

Forest Frederick Edward Yeo-Thomas was born in 1901 and had fought in the First World War, as well as for the Poles against the Russians in 1919 when he escaped captivity the day before he was due to be shot. At the onset of the Second World War he was working as the director of the Parisian dressmaking company Molyneux.

At 38 years old, Yeo-Thomas only got his chance to join the RAF by persistence, but was soon in a liaison role thanks to his fluency in French. After his commission, he was to transfer to SOE's RF Section, which worked closely with de Gaulle's Free French.

Forest 'the white rabbit' Yeo-Thomas, one of SOE's most successful agents, lived at Queen Court on Guildford Street.

Yeo-Thomas was, after numerous missions to occupied France, finally captured by the Gestapo in 1944. The circumstances that led up to his arrest were an unfortunate mix of bad luck and circumstance. RF Section had, for some time, been trying to extract two agents from France, Brossolette and Bollaert. Bad weather had continually prevented them from flying out, so they opted to travel by sea. Unfortunately, once in Brittany they were picked up by a routine patrol simply because they did not have the correct papers for that particular region.

For a month the Gestapo had no idea of the value of the people they were holding, but finally Brossolette and Bollaert were betrayed. Meanwhile, Yeo-Thomas, believing their identities were still unknown to the Gestapo and that they were still in Rennes Prison, was making plans for their escape. Yeo-Thomas was picked up by the Gestapo after his contact failed to show at a meeting on the Paris Metro. After being tortured for information he would not reveal about the French Resistance, he was sent to Buchenwald to be executed, where he was to make the most improbable of escapes. With the war drawing to an end, he persuaded a German that he would testify on his behalf at any subsequent war trial if he helped him to escape (and he was good to his word), eventually meeting up with American forces at Chemnitz in eastern Germany.

At the end of the war Yeo-Thomas finally got the Military Cross he had been recommended for earlier to go alongside the *Croix de Guerre* with Palms already awarded to him. He was an important witness at the Nuremberg War Trials, identifying Buchenwald guards from his imprisonment there. He died in Paris in 1964, aged 61.

Royal Canadian Air Force Headquarters
20 LINCOLN'S INN FIELDS

Tube: Holborn
Barclays Cycle Hire: Sardinia Street, Holborn

LINCOLN'S INN FIELDS can be found tucked in between High Holborn and Kingsway and can be accessed from either of those streets by one of the many alleyways. No. 20 can be found at the eastern end of the street.

Canada was one of Britain's most faithful allies during the Second World War, declaring war on Germany on 10 September 1939, just seven days after Britain and France. Canadian troops fought alongside the British for the duration of the conflict from the beginning, with the 1st Canadian Division heading to France in the second BEF.

The Royal Canadian Air Force building in Lincoln's Inn Fields, with the memorial to those who served in front.

In the early days of the war, one of Canada's first contributions was with pilots and planes to help fight in the Battle of Britain and to increase Bomber Command's resources. In all, the Royal Canadian Air Force had forty-eight squadrons based in the UK and supplied men to many RAF units around the country. The Canadian Royal Air Force set up its own headquarters at 20 Lincoln's Inn Fields, supporting the 85,000 Canadians working in the RCAF, of whom 14,455 died during the course of the war.

The building is marked by a small memorial directly in front of it, in the field itself, while a Canadian maple tree was planted in 1999 to further commemorate those who lost their lives during the war.

The area of London known as the City is centred around the Bank of England on Threadneedle Street and is the financial heart of London. To the west of the bank is St Paul's Cathedral, which was to become a potent symbol of Britain's ability to endure the Blitz, surviving thanks to the dedication of the St Paul's Watch and some good fortune.

In 1939, to the east of the City the Royal Mint could still be found overlooking the Tower of London while, just past the Tower, the first of London's dockyards started with St Katharine Dock. The wharves of these docks made up the Port of London – the biggest port in the world at the time. The massive basins, linked by canals, covered an extraordinary area on the north bank of the Thames. They stretched from just beyond the Tower to the Isle of Dogs and continued on to the impressive Victoria and Albert Docks.

These docks were one of the Luftwaffe's primary targets and were easily hit, even by the inaccurate bombers of the time. Fires raged as the vast array of goods in dockside warehouses burned, marking them out for future raiders. Fires at St Katharine Docks erupted when warehouses containing paraffin wax and fat were hit, the concoction floating on the water's surface, burning freely. The docks were bombed over and over, but any bombs that were released too late to fall on the docks came crashing down on the City, making it one of the most bombed areas of London, with entire streets laid to ruin.

While the City is still a financial centre, the Docklands have changed immeasurably since the war with the Canary Wharf development.

St Paul's Cathedral still dominates the London skyline today as it did during the Blitz.

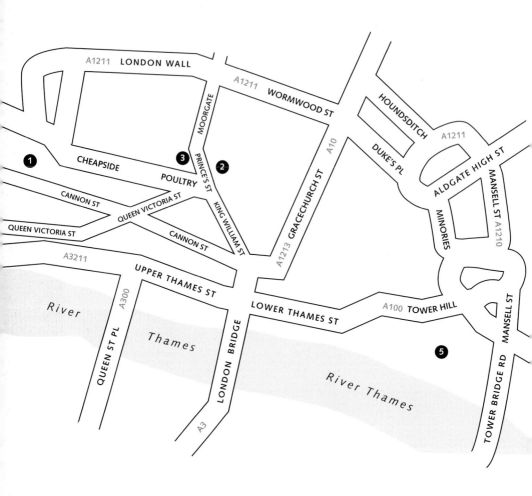

KEY

1. St Paul's Cathedral
2. Bank of England
3. Caisse Centrale de la France
4. Royal Mint
5. Tower of London

St Paul's Cathedral
ST PAUL'S CHURCHYARD

Tube: St Paul's
Barclays Cycle Hire: Godliman Street, St Paul's

St Paul's Cathedral can be found in between Newgate Street and ST PAUL'S CHURCHYARD and is a short walk up from the northern bank of the Thames where the Millennium Bridge ends.

The cathedral, as it stands today, was designed by Christopher Wren to replace the building destroyed in the Great Fire of London. The last stone was laid in 1708, completing one of London's most iconic buildings. At the height of the Blitz, St Paul's dominated the skyline to an ever-greater extent as neighbouring streets were destroyed. With its surroundings being ground away by the Luftwaffe's bombs, the fate of the cathedral became more and more symbolic.

The survival of the cathedral was in part down to good luck such as on the night of 10 October 1940, when a bomb penetrated the roof leaving a crater in the north transept, but causing little real damage. Then, on 12 September another bomb landed in Dean's Yard, cleaving through the soil and coming to rest by the foundations of the cathedral itself. For almost three days bomb

St Paul's Cathedral still standing, surrounded by ruins, having survived the Blitz. © TfL from the London Transport Museum

Bomb damage to the statue of John Milton that stood outside the City of London church in which he is buried.

disposal teams dug down to reach the bomb, discovering that it had fractured a gas pipe and severed electrical cables along the way. Fitted with a Type 17 fuse, which was designed to trip anytime up to seventy-two hours after being dropped, there was no time left to defuse it where it lay. The bomb was loaded on to a truck and driven to Hackney Marshes where it was detonated in safety.

However, there was nothing lucky about the dedication, hard work and bravery of the St Paul's Watch. Made up of 300 members, with forty on duty every night, they looked after the cathedral during the nightly bombing raids. St Paul's was bombed repeatedly and the night of 29 December 1940 alone, twenty-eight fire bombs fell on and around the building. But, thanks to the St Paul's Watch on duty that night, the cathedral survived as they managed to extinguish them all before the fires could spread.

The whole area around St Paul's was decimated by Luftwaffe bombs with much of the area being razed to the ground, but St Paul's remained more or less intact. With victory declared on 8 May 1945, ten services for peace were held consecutively, each attended by more than 3,000 people. Then, in 1965, a state funeral was held for Churchill at St Paul's.

St Paul's can be visited from Monday to Saturday by the public, with entry available to the main cathedral floor, the crypt and the three galleries.

Bank of England
THREADNEEDLE STREET

Tube: Bank
Docklands Light Railway: Bank
Barclays Cycle Hire: Bank of England Museum, Bank

The Bank of England, created by Royal Charter in 1694, has been located in the heart of the City on THREADNEEDLE STREET since 1734. Over time, the bank moved away from commercial business to take on the role of a central bank responsible for monetary and financial stability.

As Hitler's armies overran mainland Europe, the threat of invasion was very real. As with other countries, it was clear that the invading Nazis would appropriate everything of value to their cause. So, in the first instance, 2,000 tons of gold was physically moved out of harm's way and transported to Canada. Once safely there, the Bank of England staff had the unenviable problem of managing a wartime economy.

The Bank of England was extremely vulnerable, being in one of the most heavily bombed areas of Britain. The bank itself had a very near miss

A fake £5 note produced by prisoners in Scahsenhausen concentration camp, and the blue, rather than green, £1 note.

when a bomb hit the road junction in front of their building, destroying Bank Underground station and killing fifty-eight people. Eventually the bank moved its entire operation to Overton, a small town in Hampshire, where it could carry out its work in safety for the remainder of the war.

The bank faced many challenges throughout the war, first of which was the scarcity of raw materials. A lack of green ink, for example, meant that pound notes turned blue as of 1940, not returning back to the traditional green until 1948. There was also Operation Bernhard, the German plan to flood the British economy with fake notes of £1, £5, £10 and £20 denominations, to contend with. In Block 19 at Sachsenhausen concentration camp, prisoners were forced to use their skills to produce millions of pounds' worth of fake notes. Aware of the plan, the Bank of England believed that security measures would stop the notes getting into circulation but still issued a warning about counterfeits, put an import ban on pound notes and stopped printing the large white £5 notes altogether. Pound notes were widely used in Europe where it was an 'international' currency and many fakes entered common use, but few of the 'white notes' made it into circulation.

The Bank of England is still located on Threadneedle Street complete with a small museum, the entrance to which can be found on Bartholomew Lane.

Caisse Centrale de la France Libre
9 PRINCES STREET

Tube: Bank
Docklands Light Railway: Bank
Barclays Cycle Hire: Bank of England Museum, Bank

PRINCES STREET can be found in the City of London and runs along one side of the Bank of England. No. 9 was probably situated where the modern bank building is at No. 8.

Initially, de Gaulle had few men, women and resources available to run and maintain the Free French government. Gradually, as more and more dedicated people managed to flee France their numbers swelled, but to make them a viable organisation they required resources and infrastructure, one of the key requirements of which was a banking system.

The Bank of England began providing financial resources from as early as August 1940, only a few months after the evacuation from Dunkirk, with the British government lending the French funds that were to be repaid after the war. The bank then helped create the Caisse Centrale de la France Libre (CCFL), the Bank of the Free French, which began operating from 9 Princes Street in December 1941. With André Diethelm as its first director general,

Princes Street where the Bank of the Free French, the Caisse Centrale de la France Libre was set up with help from the Bank of England.

the CCFL became the 'note issuer and national treasury of de Gaulle's Free France' (www.bankofengland.co.uk).

Diethelm was soon looking further afield to the French colonies in West Africa. One of the primary causes of concern was the right of a bank located in Vichy France to issue notes that could be circulated in the African colonies. The problem was inflation; notes circulated in Vichy-controlled Africa, where inflation was high, could be smuggled into Free French African countries where the franc circulated at a fixed rate to sterling, to be exchanged on favourable terms, potentially harming the British economy. The solution was simple: the replacement of all coins and notes with a new design, which happened in 1942.

Towards the end of 1943 the CCFL moved to Algiers, where it was renamed the Caisse Centrale de la France d'Outre-mer. It still exists today as the Caisse de Développement, with its focus now being on poverty alleviation.

Royal Mint
ROYAL MINT COURT, TOWER HILL

Tube: Tower Hill
Barclays Cycle Hire: Tower Gardens, Tower

The site of the old Royal Mint is now referred to as ROYAL MINT COURT, the entrance to which can be found off Tower Hill, which is behind the north-east corner of the Tower of London.

The first Royal Mint was built in the Tower of London but, as demand increased, it was decided to move it to new, purpose-built accommodation. The site chosen was on the nearby Little Tower Hill and began operating around 1810. Come the Second World War, the Royal Mint was still producing money from this same building.

Despite a war being on, there was still an urgent need to produce hard currency to ensure people were paid. It was recognised that if the mint was bombed there could be a serious interruption to the production of coinage. While it does not appear to have caused major disruption, a bomb did hit the mint on 8 December 1940, killing three people who worked there. However, to ensure that there would be no long-term interruption, an auxiliary mint was set up at Pinewood Studios for the duration of the war.

When decimalisation took place in the 1970s, the mint moved all its operations to Wales. The building at Royal Mint Court is now a serviced office centre.

The Royal Mint produced coinage from its London building on Tower Hill but set up alternative facilities at Pinewood Film Studios.

Tower of London
TOWER HILL

Tube: Tower Hill
Barclays Cycle Hire: Tower Gardens, Tower

The Tower of London is one of the city's most recognisable landmarks, sitting on the northern bank of the Thames. The Tower has St Katherine Marina, which was part of the Docklands, to one side, the City to the other and is overlooked by HMS *Belfast* from the Thames

On 10 May 1941 Rudolf Hess, unbeknown to Hitler, flew his Messerschmitt Bf 110 towards Scotland on a personal mission to sue for peace. On his arrival, Hess was taken from Scotland to the Tower of London while a somewhat surprised Secret Intelligence Service worked out what to do with him. Hess's stay at the Tower was brief, as he was soon transferred to Mytchett Place, or Camp Z, near Aldershot, which had been specially prepared with microphones to record his every word.

Hess was one of Hitler's closest confidants, having been imprisoned with him in the 1920s. It was during this time in prison that Hitler wrote *Mein Kampf*, much of it being dictated to Hess. As such, Hess was considered one of the most senior figures in the Nazi party behind Hitler, so his arrival in Britain was somewhat of a coup for the British and an embarrassment to the Nazis. However, despite his seniority, it soon became clear that he was not as informed about Nazi war plans as might have been expected.

Rudolph Hess's prison, the Tower of London, before he was moved to 'Camp Z' near Aldershot.

Whether Hess was entirely sane has been much debated, but it does seem to be the case that he genuinely believed he could broker a peace with Britain, if only he could get an audience with the king and have the Churchill government overthrown. He intended to do this via the Duke of Hamilton, whom he had met several years previously, and who was indeed a close friend of the king. The meeting, of course, was never permitted to happen and Hess spent the rest of the war at Camp Z, being its only prisoner.

After the war he faced trial at Nuremburg where he was given life imprisonment. In 1987 he committed suicide aged 93, having spent forty-two years in Spandau Prison, twenty-one of those as its only inmate.

Docklands
DOCKLANDS

Tube: Canary Wharf
Docklands Light Railway: Canary Wharf
Barclays Cycle Hire: Jubilee Plaza, Canary Wharf

The most central area of the DOCKLANDS is focused on Canary Wharf at the northern end of the Isle of Dogs and is very well serviced by the Underground, Docklands Light Railway and multiple cycle hire racks.

London's importance as a major trading city dates back to Roman times, and as its importance grew throughout the years, so did its appetite for trade. By the end of the eleventh century the Normans had begun to develop London's docks, where trade was booming. By the outbreak of the Second World War, the Docklands covered a phenomenal area of London with several enclosed

St Katherine Docks, which was set ablaze as a mix of paraffin wax and fat burnt on the water's surface.

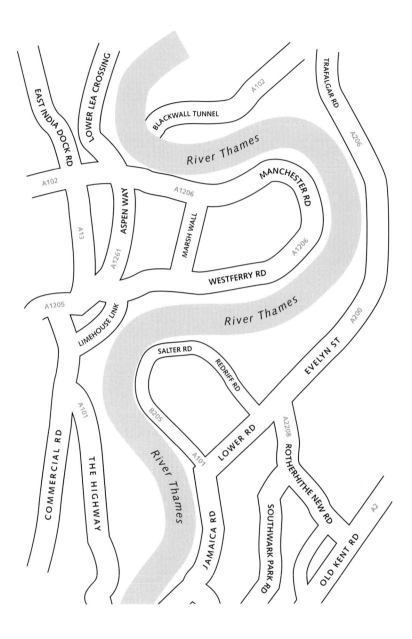

docks being used for the loading and unloading of goods. All of this was managed by the Port of London Authority (PLA), an organisation placed in charge of all of London's enclosed docks in 1930. In 1939 the London docks were handling 38 per cent of all Britain's seaborne trade and were at times hard-pressed to cope with all the material coming in.

The first change seen in the docks when Britain declared war was the appropriating of numerous wharves and ships by the military, which

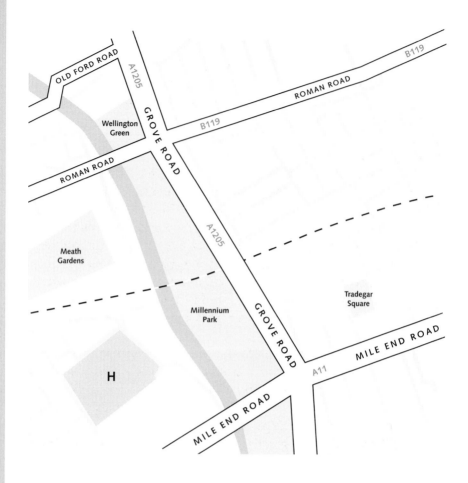

immediately made it harder to find space to unload other goods. In the early months of the war little happened in London and it was not until September 1940 that the German offensive against the city began in earnest. London, and the Docklands, had already experienced aerial bombing from Zeppelins in the First World War. These raids caused great damage and killed many, but were nothing compared to what London was about to face.

The Luftwaffe's bombing campaign had the Docklands as one of its main targets. Using the River Thames to guide them into London, it was then a relatively easy task for the Luftwaffe pilots to pick out the sprawling mass of the London Docklands. This was something that did not take much imagination to realise. As Churchill recalled, 'the German Air Force however had still as their target the Port of London, all that immense line of docks with their masses of shipping, and the largest city in the world, which did not require much accuracy to hit.' The whole area had built up into a dense mass of docks, wharves for unloading goods, factories for processing raw materials directly from the ships, associated trades, as well as densely packed housing for the thousands of people employed there. Canning Town, Millwall, Silvertown and Wapping were some of the Dockland communities that were gradually being reduced to rubble by the nightly bombing raids. In some areas, such as the Millwall Docks, the warehousing was all but totally flattened.

The firefighters returned night after night to deal with the continual blazes, made worse when warehouses containing anything from chemicals, sugar or wood to oils, wax and alcohol were set alight by high-explosive or incendiary bombs.

While the residents of the Docklands survived the Blitz of 1940–41 and the Baby Blitz – a second period of intense bombing in early 1944 – they were again in the front line when V1s and V2s were directed towards London. Fortunately the Allied armies were able to bring the war to its conclusion before these terrible weapons could inflict crippling damage to the city and its docks.

After the war the Docklands were rebuilt and enjoyed a buoyant trade for many years, remaining the most important docks in the country. However, by the late sixties they were in decline and in 1968 both the London and St Katherine Docks were closed, with the West India, Millwall and other docks soon following.

By the 1980s, this vast area, which was so critical in landing vital supplies and processing them during the war and which was so badly bombed, was a wasteland. Taking over control of the land, the London Docklands Development Corporation looked for ideas to redevelop the area, initially concentrating on the Isle of Dogs and eventually deciding on the scheme located at Canary Wharf, so called because of the imports from the Canary Islands. This vast business sector is now the commercial centre of the City, much like the docks were in the past.

First London V1 Strike
GROVE ROAD

Tube: Mile End
Barclays Cycle Hire: Antill Road, Mile End

GROVE ROAD goes through Mile End in Tower Hamlets and has Victoria Park at its northern end and Mile End Underground station at its southern end. The bridge that the first V1 struck is marked by a blue plaque.

As the Allied forces overran Europe, the ability of Germany to strike at London with massed air raids declined, as not only were the Germans losing pilots, but they were losing the airfields they had been using in France. While bombing raids still occurred, they were not anywhere near the scale of the Blitz. It was now that the Nazis were to use the first of their Vengeance weapons, the V1.

An increasing amount of effort had been put into the development of the V1, and much hope was pinned on its success. The V1 was a pilotless plane carrying explosives that was launched from special ramps directed towards England or Belgium. Once launched they would head for their target using a crude autopilot system. They would plummet to the ground when their pulse jet engine cut out, detonating on impact. The first V1 to hit London landed next to a railway bridge crossing Grove Road in the early hours of 13 June 1944, killing six and causing considerable damage.

Londoners were soon on the lookout for the arrival of these new machines, which were given the name 'doodlebugs', and soon sixty to a hundred flying bombs were heading towards London a day. The population felt they had little or no defence against such an indiscriminate weapon that could arrive any time, night or day, and there was a significant risk to morale. With the Blitz there was some sense of order, during which bombs arrived over night but the daylight hours were relatively safe. The V1 arrived any time and paralysed people could only stop and watch its descent, listening to the ear-splitting shriek, all the while hoping it would not land on their homes.

However, RAF pilots soon started to score several successes shooting V1s down, especially with high-speed planes that were able to outpace the V1. The more daring pilots manoeuvred their wing underneath that of the V1 and tried to divert its course. At the same time, General Pile, who was responsible for Britain's ground-based anti-aircraft defences, had set up a 'gun belt' to intercept the V1s heading towards London.

Meanwhile, Eisenhower's armies were gradually overrunning the launching ramps and pushing the front line back so that these weapons could not reach London. Reconnaissance Spitfires of the RAF, fitted with cameras, were hunting out the launch ramps, many cunningly camouflaged. The RAF's photographic section would inspect the images and when a launch ramp was discovered send out a bombing raid to destroy it. While the Germans were ever more ingenious in their efforts to hide the launch ramps, the people looking for them got all the better at spotting the tell-tale signs.

Eventually the V1 menace was neutralised, with the last being launched on 1 September 1944, after 2,300 had fallen on London, killing 6,184 people and seriously wounding a further 17,981. Unfortunately the even deadlier V2 rocket was being prepared by the Nazis, using much of lessons learnt from the V1; the V2 would spread further terror throughout the capital.

The boroughs of Southwark, Lambeth and Wandsworth lie east to west on the southern side of the Thames. This whole area of London was badly damaged during the Blitz as the Luftwaffe attempted to destroy the industrial areas that lined the Thames, with Battersea power station, gasworks and factories being key targets on the southern side.

The London dockyards were some of the busiest in the world and, as such, the docks both north and south of the Thames were high-priority targets for the Luftwaffe, with the Victoria and Albert Docks and the industrial areas on the northern side and the Surrey Commercial Docks on the southern side. In 1939, the banks of the Thames looked much different compared to now. Instead of the cafes, restaurants and modern apartments, the Southern bank of the Thames was lined with loading wharves, factories and other industrial buildings. Behind these could be found tightly packed housing and close-knit communities which provided the labour for the hive of industry found along the river. Inevitably, a large number of bombs missed their targets and hit residential areas causing massive damage and casualties amongst the local population.

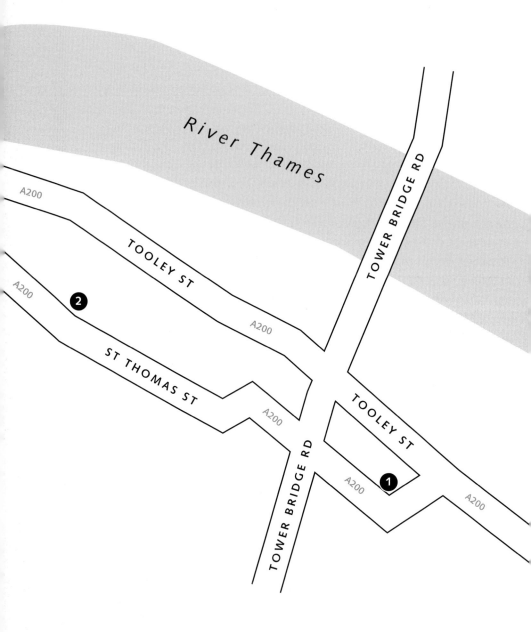

KEY
1. Druid Street Arch
2. Stainer Street

Surrey Commercial Docks, Southwark
SURREY QUAYS ROAD

Tube: Canada Water
Docklands Light Railway: Canada Water
Barclays Cycle Hire: None close

Surrey Commercial Docks could be found in the Rotherhithe area of London, on an area of land surrounded on three sides by the meandering Thames.

The land on which the Surrey Commercial Docks grew up was traditionally marshy and not considered suitable for building on. It was around 1700 that the first dock, the Great Wet Dock (later renamed Greenland Dock) was built. Over the next 200 years the docks continued to expand until there were ten of them, the last of which to be built was Quebec Dock, opened in 1926. At their height, these docks covered around 370 acres, had a storage capacity for 35,000 tonnes of grain and had 46 acres of timber storage sheds.

These stores were vital to Britain's war effort as the flow of raw materials into the country reduced due to German U-boat activity. The Luftwaffe identified Surrey Commercial Docks as a high-priority target, knowing that its destruction would be a serious blow to Britain's supply lines. Its sprawling docks were easily seen from the air and on the night of 7 September 1940 the inevitable raid came.

In preparation for a possible fire in the timber yards during peacetime, Pageants Wharf Fire Station had been built next to the Lavender Pond entrance within the docks and, on the evening of 7 September, an 'air-raid warning red' was received by the station. Looking south across the Thames, Station Officer 'Gerry' Knight and his team saw bombers hitting their targets north of the Thames and continued to watch as a detachment of bombers broke off and headed directly for the Surrey Commercial Docks.

Hay's Galleria, previously known as Hay's Wharf, in Southwark, was bombed during the war.

The bombers released their incendiary, high-explosive and oil bombs, and within a few minutes the docks were ablaze. Station Officer Knight called the watch room at Pageants Wharf Fire Station to tell Betty Barrett, who was on duty, 'send all the bloody pumps you've got; the whole bloody world's on fire!' (*The London Blitz, A Fireman's Tale*, Demarne, 1991)

He was not wrong; as fires took hold all around the firemen, it became immediately apparent that it would be impossible to contain the blaze with the scant resources on hand. Reinforcements continued to arrive throughout the night and the firemen set to work tackling the fires. They fought the fire in occasionally surreal conditions as wooden roadblocks heated up and ignited, telegraph poles spontaneously burst into flame and a determined enemy continued with their bombardment. By the end of the night over 1,000 pumps and crews had been at work trying to bring the Surrey Docks conflagration – probably the biggest of the war where half a mile of the Surrey shore was aflame – under control. Before the fire could be tamed, around 350,000 tons of timber had been consumed by the flames.

Tragically, Station Officer Gerry Knight, one of the first senior officers to attend the Surrey Commercial Docks fire, was killed the following night when he was hit by a bomb, his body only identifiable by his boots.

The change in shipping practices to the container system brought an abrupt end to the docks as they were unable to cope with the size of the new container ships, and the Surrey Commercial Docks ceased operating in December 1970. The area went into decline, with the majority of the docks being filled in and housing taking their place. This development culminated in the Docklands regeneration programme of the 1980s and the renaming of the docks to Surrey Quays, so that nowadays little remains of what were some of the busiest docks in the world.

A blue plaque commemorating these events can be found on the old dock office building on Surrey Quay Road in the Canada Water area.

Druid Street Arch
DRUID STREET

Tube: London Bridge
Barclays Cycle Hire: Tanner Street, Bermondsey

Druid Street Arch can be found just south-west of London Bridge station, on the corner of Tanner Street and DRUID STREET, and is underneath the railway tracks leading to London Bridge station.

By the end of October 1940 the Blitz was well under way, with raids occurring nightly, and Londoners were getting used to its regularity. Some people took a fatalistic approach and did not seek shelter on the basis that if they were going to be killed then there was little they could do about it. However, most people sought protection in either private shelters or in both official and unofficial communal public shelters.

Tragedies were bound to occur since there were very few truly bombproof shelters in London. The Druid Street Arch incident was one such misfortune, which was made worse by the large group of people congregating in one place. On the night of 25 October 1940, when the air-raid warnings sounded, people headed to the arch for shelter. Unfortunately it took a direct hit and the seventy-seven people there were killed. This event has been commemorated with a blue plaque.

Stainer Street
STAINER STREET

Tube: London Bridge
Barclays Cycle Hire: Hop Exchange, the Borough

STAINER STREET is actually a tunnel, which can be found running beneath London Bridge station connecting Tooley Street and St Thomas Street.

As the Blitz intensified, Londoners were forced to use any shelter available. The widespread practice of using Underground stations is well known, but soon any convenient location that offered a degree of protection was being employed as a shelter.

It is easy to see why the long Stainer Street tunnel would have been considered a safe haven from the bombs raining down on London. The long stretch of road is covered by railway tracks and, in common with most shelters, offered excellent protection against all but a direct strike. But, in February 1941, Stainer Street did take a direct hit and the bomb, which penetrated

the roof, killed sixty-eight of the people taking shelter below. A blue plaque on the southern end of the tunnel commemorates those who lost their lives in this tragedy.

The entrance to the Stainer Street tunnel and the blue plaque remembering those unfortunate enough to lose their lives when a bomb exploded on those sheltering below.

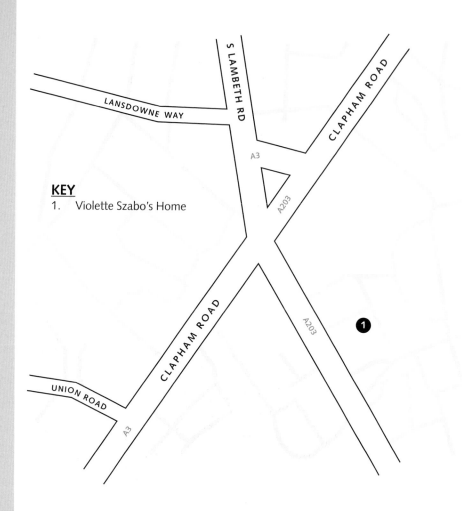

KEY
1.   Violette Szabo's Home

Violette Szabo's Home
18 BURNLEY ROAD, STOCKWELL

Tube: Stockwell
Barclays Cycle Hire: None close

No. 18 BURNLEY ROAD, the childhood home of SOE agent Violette Szabo, can be found south of the Thames, near Stockwell Underground station. This privately owned property is marked by a blue plaque.

Violette Bushell was born on 26 June 1921 in Paris, her French mother Reine Leroy having met Charles Bushell while he was serving in France during the First World War. The Bushell family then flitted between France and England for several years before finally settling in Brixton in 1932, at 12 Stockwell Park Walk. They moved to 18 Burnley Road three years later.

At the outbreak of the Second World War Violette was 18, and only 19 when she met Etienne Szabo of the French Foreign Legion, taking him home to Burnley Road to meet her parents. Within a few weeks Etienne and Violette were married, just before Etienne departed to fight the Italians. Etienne had only one homecoming before being killed during the opening engagements of the Battle of El Alamein. Heartbreakingly, Violette had their baby, Tania, without Etienne ever having seen his daughter.

This was to be the turning point of Violette's life that would ultimately lead to her own death as she resolved 'to do more – much more in this war' (*Carve Her Name With Pride*, Minney, 1989). She was to get her opportunity when talent spotters passed on her details to the Special Operations Executive. As a

The home of Violette Szabo in Burnley Road, with its blue plaque visible.

Violette Szabo.

native French speaker, her talents were much in demand and she soon found herself having an interview with a 'Mr Potter' at 3 Great Smith Street (see Victoria Hotel, p. 128). Neglecting to mention at first that she had a child, Violette was soon enrolled into SOE.

Her induction took her to many of SOE's country training schools around Britain where she learnt the skills necessary to be an SOE agent operating in France, from weapons training to parachute jumping and counter-surveillance techniques. Six weeks before D-Day, Szabo was sent on her first mission to Normandy in France. Here she pieced together what had happened to a resistance group, eventually discovering that ninety of its ninety-eight members had been arrested.

The morning after D-Day Szabo went back to France with three other SOE operatives on a mission that Buckmaster, the head of F Section responsible for sending agents into France, acknowledged would be far more dangerous than the first. Their objective was to help organise a local French resistance group, the Maquis, for operations against the Germans ahead of the Allied advance.

It was decided that the Maquis would attack a German division that would be passing through their area to reinforce their comrades defending the

Normandy beaches. Key to this was passing the information from one group to the next until the plan of attack was known by all the Maquis groups in the area. Szabo was chosen for this task, accompanied by a man called Anastasie, who would introduce her to the first Maquis group.

Disaster was to strike though as, on their way to the meeting, they were ambushed. A fierce battle followed in which Szabo ensured Anastasie's escape by hiding him under a log pile, before being captured herself, having killed several German soldiers in the fight.

Szabo was then to endure several months' imprisonment. During this time Violette was sent to the Gestapo building on Avenue Foch in Paris, where she was tortured; nonetheless, she never talked. Though she was moved several times, Szabo spent much of her captivity in Ravensbrück concentration camp where, only a few weeks before the end of the war, she was executed along with two other female agents.

Violette Szabo was posthumously awarded the George Cross – the first woman to receive that honour – and the *Croix de Guerre*. It is her image that was used on the SOE memorial, which can be found on the grass in between Lambeth Palace and the Thames (see p. 205).

Kennington Park

KENNINGTON PARK ROAD, LAMBETH

Tube: Oval
Barclays Cycle Hire: Kenning Road Post Office, Oval

Kennington Park can be found in the borough of Lambeth near to the Surrey County Cricket Ground, the Oval and Oval Underground station.

With the prospect of war very real in the late 1930s the government began making preparations to defend Britain's major cities from aerial bombing. One of the first considerations was the provision of shelter for civilians during bombing raids. The simplest solution was to create a trench system in any available park or piece of open land. In the Lambeth area, trench shelters could be found in Archbishop's, Brockwell, Myatts, Ruskin, Vauxhall and Kennington Parks.

These trenches were intended only as a temporary shelter – more a bolthole for those caught in the open – and it was estimated that people might only spend a maximum of three or four hours there. Once the trenches were dug, their walls were lined with wood and they were given a corrugated steel roof covered with earth. The first ones were built in a 'ladder' pattern, as was the case at Kennington Park, which was dug in 1938. Later trench shelters were constructed in a 'zig-zag' pattern, which was better able to withstand a nearby bomb blast. During the Blitz, these shelters were used well beyond the four hours intended, with local residents spending up to twelve hours squeezed into these small, cramped shelters.

It was on 15 October 1940 that disaster struck when a 50lb German bomb hit part of the Kennington Park trench shelter system. People in the trench were blown up beyond recognition or buried under the falling earth walls. Identification was impossible in many cases and only forty-eight bodies were recovered from what is believed to have been 104 victims. Eventually the rescuers had to concede defeat and that section was covered with lime and filled in. The remainder of the Kennington Park trench system was used for the rest of the war, finally being filled in 1947.

There is a memorial to the 1,560 civilians killed in the Lambeth area at Lambeth cemetery and now, unveiled in 2006, there is a memorial to the victims of Kennington Park, close to where they were killed as they took shelter from German bombs.

Wandsworth Prison
HEATHFIELD ROAD, WANDSWORTH

Tube: Clapham Junction
Train: Wandsworth Common
Barclays Cycle Hire: None close

Wandsworth Prison, which is still in operation today, can be found on HEATHFIELD ROAD, just to the west of Wandsworth Common.

The Treachery Act of 1940 was hurried through parliament as a more suitable and easier means of being able to prosecute people accused of 'treacherous actions during war time'; several people convicted under the Treachery Act were executed at Wandsworth Prison.

One of the first to be hanged at Wandsworth was George Johnson Armstrong on 10 July 1941. Armstrong had a long history of petty crime and fraudulent activities in between various jobs. He eventually found himself in America, where he sent a letter to the German Consul at Boston, offering his services as a spy. His defence that he was in fact trying to ensnare a Nazi spy ring himself was discounted and the death sentence was carried out.

One of the youngest men to face the Wandsworth Prison gallows was Duncan Scott-Ford. Scott-Ford was a seaman in the Merchant Navy aboard SS *Finland*, which in May 1942 was in Lisbon. Scott-Ford already had a chequered past which involved a conviction for forgery to pay for his Egyptian prostitute's lavish lifestyle. Once in Lisbon it seems he headed for the more dubious bars where he was taken in by German agents. After a long interview he was paid and given instructions as to the requirements of his German spymasters. Scott-Ford was eventually caught due to radio intercepts from Bletchley Park. There was little defence Scott-Ford could give, having passed on vital information about convoy routes to the Germans. He was sentenced to death and hanged at Wandsworth on 3 November 1942.

The most famous person to end up in Wandsworth was William Joyce, more commonly known as Lord Haw-Haw. Joyce had been a long-standing supporter of the Nazis, having joined the British Union of Fascists led by Mosley. Ultimately he was dropped from this organisation and formed his own party, the British National Socialist League. As this venture faltered Joyce made the decision, in August 1939, to depart for Germany. Joyce began broadcasting to Britain within twelve weeks of his arrival in Berlin with his call sign 'Germany calling, Germany calling'.

It is difficult to say for certain how Joyce's broadcasts affected British morale, but they were evidently popular, with the BBC estimating that around 6 million people were regularly tuning in to them. This was often as is it was believed he passed on information about the progress of the war, sometimes prior to the BBC. At the same time he certainly offended a good proportion of the population with his sneering, anti-semitic rhetoric.

As the war drew to a conclusion, Joyce and his wife left war-torn Berlin, eventually going into hiding in a town called Flensburg on the German–Danish border, where they were picked up by chance by two English officers. Joyce was hence returned to England to face trial for treason.

While Joyce did not deny his actions, he did deny they amounted to treason primarily because he had been born in the US and was therefore a US citizen. The case hinged on the fact that he had acquired a British passport to travel to Germany and therefore, according to the prosecution, owed allegiance to the Crown while he held this passport (before he became a naturalised German citizen). The charge that Joyce was found guilty of was that during the period of his initial broadcasts he was in possession of a valid British passport. The only evidence offered on this count was that a Special Branch detective, Albert Hunt, had heard a broadcast by Joyce in September or October 1939. This was sufficient enough for the jury, which took only twenty-three minutes to reach a guilty verdict. An appeal was dismissed and Joyce was sent to Wandsworth's gallows in the early hours of 3 January 1946.

The London Underground network's first line, the Metropolitan, opened in January 1863, followed by others soon after. By the mid-1930s all the lines, which until this point had been operated by private companies, were incorporated into one organisation: the London Transport Passenger Board (LTPB).

The Underground lines had developed over the seventy-five years prior to the outbreak of the war. However, due to competition between lines and stations, and lower than expected footfalls in some places, some stations became unprofitable and were simply closed down, many of which can still be seen today. These stations provided ready-made subterranean shelters that were pressed into immediate use, such as Brompton Road which was used as a control centre for London's anti-aircraft defences and Down Street which became the location of the temporary Cabinet Office.

The most famous wartime use of the Underground system was as air-raid shelters during the Blitz. At the outset of the war it was believed by the government that the Underground would be vital for transportation across the city. It was imagined that people sheltering there would impede the service and a ban on using Underground stations as shelters was put in place. Even Churchill seemed unsure of whether the tunnels could or could not be used as shelters, as is clear from a prime ministerial memo to Sir Edward Brides, the Home Secretary and Minister of Transport:

> When I asked the cabinet the other day why the tubes could not be used to some extent, even at the expense of transport facilities, as air-raid shelters, I was assured that this was most undesirable, and that the whole matter had been reviewed before that conclusion was reached. I now see that the Aldwych Tube is to be used as a shelter. Pray let me have more information about this, and what has happened to supersede the former decisive arguments.

The ban was lifted in September 1940, apparently after a determined group of civilians forced their way into Liverpool Street station, with one newspaper saying. 'London decided how the tube stations were to be used.' During September 1940 the number of people using the Underground as shelter reached its peak of 177,000.

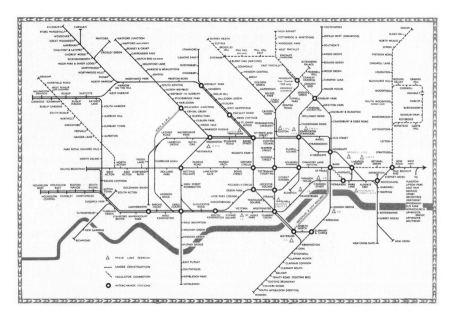

The extent of the Underground as it was in 1939. © TfL from the London Transport Museum collection

Aldwych Underground Station
SURREY STREET

Tube: Temple
Barclays Cycle Hire: Strand, Strand

Aldwych is the only station at the end of a spur off the Piccadilly line, running from Holborn. One of the original exits from the station, complete with the Aldwych Underground sign, can be found on SURREY STREET.

Aldwych station opened in November 1907 as Strand station, but was soon renamed Aldwych to avoid confusion with another stop called Strand. It ran continuously until its temporary closure for wartime use from 21 September 1940; it reopened in July 1946. London Transport agreed to the closure so that the station could be used specifically by the British Museum and the Public Records Office. The British Museum used it as a storage facility for some of its artefacts, including the Elgin Marbles, which stayed there until 1948.

As the Blitz wore on it was agreed that Aldwych could be used as a public air-raid shelter, something it was ideally suited to since trains no longer ran there. On at least one occasion during the war the station hosted entertainment put on by the Entertainments National Service Association (ENSA), where the shelterers sat on the tracks as the ENSA troupe performed on the platform.

The disused entrance to Aldwych underground station on Surrey Street, one of the first to be used as an air-raid shelter during the war.

Today Aldwych no longer functions as an operational Underground station, with the last passenger-carrying train running on 20 September 1994. However, the station is much in demand as a film location and has been used in many films set during the Second World War, including *The Battle of Britain* and, more recently, *Atonement*.

Bank Underground Station
CORNHILL

Tube: Bank
Docklands Light Railway: Bank
Barclays Cycle Hire: Bank of England Museum, Bank

Bank station can be found on the Northern line and Central line, one stop on from St Paul's. There is also an interconnect with Monument station (via escalator link, according to the 1938 Underground map). The station itself lies beneath the intersection of CORNHILL, Threadneedle Street, Prince's Street, King William Street and Queen Victoria Street, and draws its name from its proximity to the Bank of England.

In January 1941, a bomb landed with sufficient force to penetrate the road intersection above the station, causing massive damage and fifty-eight deaths. The driver of a train travelling towards the station was reportedly blown out of his seat while people waiting on the platform were said to have been thrown, by the force of the explosion, into the path of the oncoming train.

The massive crater left after a bomb struck the road junction above Bank Underground station, killing fifty-eight people. The exposed station platform, complete with advertising hoardings, can be seen as the clean-up effort begins. © TfL from the London Transport Museum

The crater left by the bomb was enormous and exposed the entire Bank station booking hall, leaving the biggest bomb crater in London, which had to be temporally spanned by engineers using a Bailey bridge.

Bethnal Green Underground Station
CAMBRIDGE HEATH ROAD

Tube: Bethnal Green
Barclays Cycle Hire: Bethnal Green Gardens, Bethnal Green

Bethnal Green Underground station can be found at the eastern end of the Central line, with its main entrance on CAMBRIDGE HEATH ROAD. It was the scene of the worst civilian disaster of the Second World War and was all the more tragic as it was not directly caused by German bombing.

Before the night-time raids began, civilians would form orderly queues, filing into the stations for shelter when they were opened. On 3 March 1943 such a queue had formed outside Bethnal Green station. Although the exact cause could never be determined, it has been speculated that anti-aircraft gun and rocket fire from nearby Victoria Park caused the crowd to panic and surge forward into the station. A young mother tripped near the foot of the stairwell causing a crush in which 173 people lost their lives, although the woman and her child survived. This disaster was kept from the public as government officials feared that it might have a negative impact on morale on the Home Front.

Bethnal Green Underground station is still in use today and a plaque can be found at the station remembering those who lost their lives in the disaster.

Balham Underground Station

BALHAM HIGH ROAD

Tube: Balham
Barclays Cycle Hire: None close

Balham Underground station can be found in the borough of Wandsworth, south of the Thames, on the Northern line between Clapham South and Tooting Bec. The station's main entrance is on the corner of BALHAM HIGH ROAD and Balham Station Road.

Like virtually every other on the Underground network, Balham was used by hundreds of people every night to shelter from German bombing raids. The risk, always present, was that one 'lucky' bomb would cause significant casualties. The bomb that hit Balham High Road, which is only about 9m above Balham station, ruptured a water main which flooded the station. Of the 600 people packed in that evening, around 500 managed to crawl to safety via an emergency hatch opened by an LTPB employee. However, sixty-eight people lost their lives from the explosion, falling rubble and drowning

The bomb that fell on Balham High Road killed sixty-eight people sheltering in the Underground station below. The crater left behind was big enough to swallow the bus being driven by Albert Coe. © TfL from the London Transport Museum

in this incident – seeing a greater loss of life than most single incidents in London. The crater left by the Balham bomb was extensive, being of sufficient size to destroy the buildings alongside it and swallow an entire bus. The bus was being driven by Albert Coe, who miraculously survived the experience.

Balham station is still in use today and a plaque can be found on the wall, just before passing through the ticket barriers used to exit the station, commemorating the incident and those who lost their lives.

Borough Underground Station
BOROUGH HIGH STREET

Tube: Borough
Barclays Cycle Hire: Borough High Street, The Borough

Borough Underground station can be found south of the Thames on the corner of BOROUGH HIGH STREET and Great Dover Street.

Once the use of the Underground as public air-raid shelters was authorised, Borough station was modified to allow more people to enter the station platforms. New staircases were constructed to a tube spur that could accommodate up to 14,000 people. There is a plaque on the side of the station that details this wartime addition to the station's facilities.

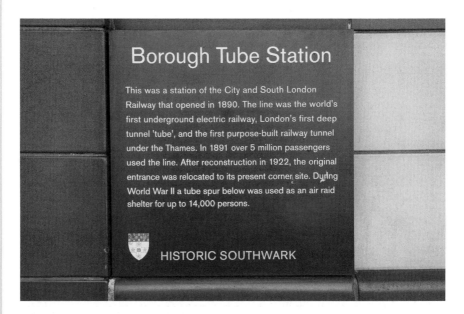

The plaque outside Borough Underground station noting its wartime conversion.

Trafalgar Square Underground Station
STRAND

Tube: Charing Cross
Barclays Cycle Hire: Craven Street, Strand

During the Second World War, Trafalgar Square Underground station could be found on the Bakerloo line and was the stop before Piccadilly Circus. The station was also at the northern end of a tunnel network built under Whitehall to protect vital communication links, a project known as 'Post Office scheme 2845'. An access shaft, later upgraded to house a lift, was built up to the Trafalgar Square station. While primarily intended to protect communication links during the Blitz, it also served as a protected route for staff to move between government buildings, especially after major extensions carried out in 1941 which linked the tunnel all the way to the Cabinet War Rooms.

Trafalgar Square Underground station was also used as a public air-raid shelter. On 12 October 1940 seven people were killed while sheltering in the station when a bomb hit Trafalgar Square near the King Charles I statue. The bomb burrowed its way through the ground exploding in the station itself.

Today, Trafalgar Square station no longer appears on the London Underground map after it was amalgamated with the Strand station on the Northern line into Charing Cross station in the 1970s.

Down Street Underground Station
DOWN STREET

Tube: Hyde Park Corner
Barclays Cycle Hire: Wellington Arch, Hyde Park

Down Street Underground station is located on the Piccadilly line between Hyde Park Corner and Green Park, with the station entrance being on DOWN STREET, off Piccadilly.

Down Street had very little success as an Underground station and, with very few people using it, closed in 1932. With the threat of war looming, the station was taken over by the government for use as a temporary Cabinet office until the Cabinet Rooms were completed (see p. 105).

The War Cabinet met at Down Street Underground station on several occasions, and Churchill spent several nights in the station, which had been fitted out with a bed and bathtub (the latter of which is still there). To prevent 'German spies' on the Piccadilly line looking in as they passed by Down Street, a wall was built along the platform.

The Railway Executive Committee meeting at Down Street Underground station with Frank Pick, vice-chairman of the London Transport Passenger Board Executive, fourth from right. © TfL from the London Transport Museum

Once the Cabinet Rooms in Whitehall were completed, the prime minster and his War Cabinet stopped using the station. However, that was not the end of Down Street's role in the war. Once vacated, the station became the control centre for the entire rail network, with a staff of seventy-five working, eating and sleeping there, connected to the outside world via a small telephone exchange. The station was also used to hold meetings of the Railway Executive Committee and became their headquarters.

Today the station is one of the Underground networks famous 'ghost' stations and is only ever visited periodically by London Transport staff.

Brompton Road Underground Station
COTTAGE PLACE

Tube: Kensington
Barclays Cycle Hire: Holy Trinity Brompton, Knightsbridge

Brompton Road Underground station can be found in Kensington, the old entrance still visible from COTTAGE PLACE, not far from Harrods. The station itself is on the Piccadilly line between South Kensington and Knightsbridge. Brompton Road station had never succeeded and trains began to pass through it only a few years after it opened. It finally closed in 1934.

The onset of the Second World War brought with it a new purpose for this station as the control room for London's 1st Anti-Aircraft Division, with its subterranean location protecting the military staff from the Luftwaffe bombs.

The street-level view of Brompton Road, which was used as a command centre during the Blitz.

The platform was bricked up to create office space and one of the lift shafts was converted into four operations rooms. From here London's ground-based air defences, such as barrage balloons and the batteries at Hyde Park and Regent's Park, were controlled.

Although it is hard to substantiate, it has been rumoured that after his capture in Scotland, Rudolf Hess was taken to Brompton Road for questioning, presumably before being taken to the Tower of London.

Brompton Road station still has many of the remnants of its Second World War past, with maps of London and its air defences still hanging from the wall but, despite some entrepreneurial efforts to open it and other disused stations as restaurants, it remains closed, but has been put up or sale by the MoD in 2013.

Leicester Square Underground Station
CHARING CROSS ROAD

Tube: Leicester Square
Barclays Cycle Hire: Panton Street, West End

Leicester Square Underground station has several entrances in and around Leicester Square and CHARING CROSS ROAD, and is on the Piccadilly and Northern lines.

Towards the end of the war the Nazis began launching V-weapons against several targets including London. The first was the V1 or Doodlebug

One of the entrances to Leicester Square Underground station. From here floodgates sealing off tunnels under the Thames were operated.

(see First V1 Strike, p. 149), but this was to be replaced by the more deadly V2 rocket, the first hitting London without any warning at 6.44 p.m. on 8 September 1944.

The first and most obvious thing that could be seen was the sheer devastation that each V2 would cause. The rocket hit the ground at supersonic speeds, its massive warhead detonating to leave behind a huge crater. There was a concern that a V2 rocket landing in the Thames itself had the potential to penetrate one of the many Underground tunnels passing below.

The potential damage caused could have led to serious flooding of much of the Underground network, causing a great loss of life and incalculable damage. Fortunately, with the use of radar, it was possible for the British to detect when a V2 was launched. Leicester Square station became the control centre for co-ordinating precautionary measures to protect the Underground network from flooding. Once a warning was received, controllers at Leicester Square had four minutes to clear all trains from sections under the Thames and close the floodgates, thus isolating those sections under the Thames from the rest of the network.

While many V2s fell on London, none of them damaged the Underground train lines beneath the Thames so these defensive measures were never put to the test.

Notting Hill Gate Underground Station
NOTTING HILL GATE

Tube: Notting Hill Gate
Barclays Cycle Hire: Notting Hill Gate Station, Notting Hill

Notting Hill Gate station can be found on NOTTING HILL GATE at the end of Bayswater and is just a few minutes away from Kensington Gardens.

Notting Hill Gate station was used by the local population to shelter from the bombing overhead and, like many other stations, had its facilities improved to make their stay more comfortable.

One addition at Notting Hill Gate was a Medical Aid Station that was equipped to deal with emergency cases that might be seen. Such facilities gave the public extra reassurance that they would be safe and well looked after while sheltering in the Underground stations and that they would not have to needlessly go to the surface to look for aid.

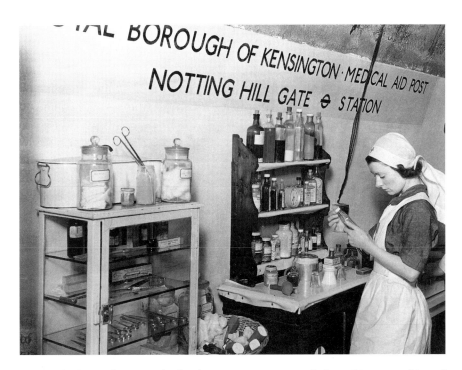

A nurse looking after a medical aid station at Notting Hill Gate. Nurses at this and other similar aid stations were ready to provide assistance to Londoners sheltering in the Underground network. © TfL from the London Transport Museum

St Mary's Underground Station
WHITECHAPEL ROAD

Tube: Whitechapel
Barclays Cycle Hire: New Road 2, Whitechapel

St Mary's Underground station opened in 1884 and closed in 1938. It could be found on the District line between Aldgate East and Whitechapel.

Soon after its closure, St Mary's reopened as a public air-raid shelter when London Transport agreed to lease the station to Stepney Borough Council. The station was used throughout the war as an air-raid shelter, despite being bombed twice, once in October 1940 and again in the spring of 1941. The second bomb destroyed a temporary entrance and most of what remained of the station at street level.

The station today has been completely abandoned and at street level there is no sign of the station's existence as all traces of the entrance hall have been destroyed by bombing. However, parts of the air-raid shelter remain underground and are still visible, such as wooden benches that line the walls and holes used to secure bunk beds. Also, the rudimentary air pumps which were used to circulate air can still be found in the station.

Camden Town Underground Station
CAMDEN HIGH STREET

Tube: Camden Town
Barclays Cycle Hire: Greenland Road, Camden Town

Camden Town Underground station is on the Northern line and can be found midway along CAMDEN HIGH STREET.

Sometime around October 1940 the station took a direct hit from a Luftwaffe bomb, destroying a third of the façade and damaging much of the station. The part of the façade that was destroyed has never been rebuilt and the name of the station, which stretched along the entire width of the original building, has been condensed into the part that remains. The damage that was repaired on the adjoining building can also be seen. This busy station is still in use today.

Camden Town Underground station with extensive damage to the station façade and adjoining building after a bomb strike in October 1940. © TfL from the London Transport Museum

The Deep Level Shelter System
CHENIES STREET

Tube: Goodge Street
Barclays Cycle Hire: Alfred Place, Bloomsbury

While the remnants of most of the Deep Level Shelters remain, one of the easiest to get to and see from street level is at CHENIES STREET, off Tottenham Court Road, very near to Goodge Street station.

The Deep Level Shelter System was commissioned in 1940 and completed in 1942. Each of the ten proposed shelters aimed to provide total protection for thousands of Londoners and vital government departments.

The shelters were to be built adjacent to existing Underground lines, with eight being on the Northern line and two on the Central line. The Deep Level Shelters on the Northern line were to be at Belsize Park, Camden Town, Goodge Street, Oval, Stockwell, Clapham North, Clapham Common and Clapham South, although construction on the shelter at Oval was abandoned at an early stage.

The appropriately named 'Eisenhower Centre' and the entrance to the Deep Level Shelter found on Chenies Street.

The Deep Level Shelters on the Central line were to be located at Chancery Lane and St Paul's; however, the works at St Paul's were stopped due to concerns that the cathedral might collapse.

Each shelter had the same basic design of two parallel tunnels 365m long split on to two levels. Those that were to be used as civilian shelters had bunks to accommodate up to 8,000 people. Large concrete structures were built at street level as entrances to the shelters, most of which can still be seen.

The shelters at Belsize Park, Camden Town, Clapham North and Clapham South were used as public air-raid shelters throughout the war, offering combined protection to 32,000 Londoners every night.

Chancery Lane and Clapham Common were designated as government citadels for use during the V1 and V2 attacks, ensuring that officials could carry on with vital war work in total safety and without interruption.

The shelter at Stockwell became home to American troops stationed in London while the shelter at Goodge Street became a command centre which was used by Generals Montgomery and Eisenhower to co-ordinate the D-Day landings on the British and Canadian beaches, Gold, Sword and Juno. The first reports from any landing beaches reportedly were heard here.

Most of the shelters are now used for data and document storage. The Goodge Street shelter, now known as the Eisenhower Centre, briefly housed West Indian immigrants arriving into the UK in 1948. The shelter at Chancery Lane was incorporated into part of British Telecom's Kingsway Telephone Exchange, a massive underground complex beneath High Holborn that housed a telephone exchange. This was built in response to the atomic threat posed by the Soviet Union in the 1950s. It is now disused and was put up for sale in 2008.

There are many memorials of remembrance around London, from the impressive Battle of Britain Memorial to simple plaques remembering those who gave their lives. Many statues have been commissioned in honour of individual soldiers and their leadership in battle, while others recognise the impact of politicians like Churchill and Roosevelt.

Many memorials acknowledge the extreme fortitude, bravery and sacrifice made by groups, honouring and remembering those who served their country. There is a monument dedicated to the London fire fighters who risked their lives during the Blitz, an impressive memorial to all those who fought in the Battle of Britain and another honouring all those who served with the Special Operations Executive.

The list is extensive, as it should be, for the sacrifice made by Britain and her allies was extraordinary. From the ordinary man and woman on the street to the royal family, men and women around the world all played their part, with millions giving their lives to ensure our future freedom.

Churchill on the steps of the Admiralty.

Viscount Alan Francis Brooke Statue
WHITEHALL

Tube: Embankment
Barclays Cycle Hire: Embankment (Horse Guards), Westminster

The statue of Field Marshal Alan Francis Brooke, 1st Viscount Alanbrooke KG, GCB, OM, GCVO, DSO & Bar can be found on Raleigh Green between those of Slim and Montgomery. Raleigh Green is on WHITEHALL next to the Ministry of Defence's main building.

General Alan Brooke was sent to France with the British Expeditionary Force (BEF) as the commander of II Corps (there was also I and III Corps, as well as an Administrative Corps, with a combined total of 316,000 men), under the overall command of Lord Gort.

Once the German offensive into Belgium and France commenced, the defence of those countries quickly turned into a rout as the Belgian and then

The statue of Alan Brooke, one of Britain's most prominent Second World War military leaders, on Whitehall.

the French armies collapsed. As the German Army advanced into France, the BEF and what remained of the French Army were squeezed into an ever-shrinking salient around Dunkirk. However, on 29 May 1940, Brooke was ordered to return to England, leaving command of II Corps to Montgomery.

The resulting evacuation via Dunkirk was not the end of British involvement in mainland Europe for 1940. Brooke was immediately sent back to command the many thousands of troops still located in north-west France. Fortunately he quickly realised the futility of these men remaining in France and told Churchill that they must be withdrawn. Despite Churchill's initial objections, he eventually acquiesced and some 200,000 men were safely returned to England.

Come July 1940, Brooke was put in command of UK Home Defences and was thus responsible for the preparation of the UK for the expected German invasion. Brooke immediately halted plans laid down by his predecessor, Ironside, who had envisaged massive static defences including 'stop' lines around London. Brooke favoured a flexible and mobile reserve who would properly engage the enemy once they had landed, with static coastal defences only aimed at holding up the initial landings, not preventing them.

Brooke was promoted to Chief of the Imperial General Staff and was chairman of the Chief of Staffs Committee, and as such was the direct advisor on military matters to the prime minister. He was promoted to field marshal in 1944.

After the war he published his war diaries which were noted for their no-nonsense assessment of the war, with criticism being laid where Brooke believed it necessary – something even Churchill did not escape.

Field Marshal Earl Alexander of Tunis Statue
BIRDCAGE WALK

Tube: St James's Park
Barclays Cycle Hire: Butler Place, Westminster

The statue of Field Marshal Earl Harold Alexander of Tunis can be found next to the Guards Chapel on BIRDCAGE WALK, opposite the Guards' Wellington Barracks.

Alexander had fought in the First World War and was involved in the Second from the earliest stage. Taking the first infantry division to France, Alexander remained until the bitter end. Once surrounded and the Dunkirk evacuation was under way, Gort, who had been in overall command of the British forces, was compelled to leave by Churchill rather than risk capture. Gort's command passed to Alexander after his initial choice, General Barker of I Corps, appeared unable to cope with the desperate situation.

Alexander successfully oversaw the Dunkirk evacuation, making many tough decisions along the way, including giving the order that 'no more stretcher cases should be evacuated' due to the amount of space they took up. Finally, Alexander, along with Bill Tennant, boarded a motor launch and toured the beaches and harbour, calling out for any soldiers who might have been left behind. Finding none, they departed, signalling the end of Operation Dynamo.

Alexander went on to have many high-level commands during the war in Burma, North Africa and the Mediterranean, where he served under Eisenhower as the commander of Allied ground forces for the invasion of Sicily. When Eisenhower returned to Europe to take command of the D-Day landings, Alexander succeeded him as Supreme Allied Commander in the Mediterranean.

Animals in War Memorial
PARK LANE

Tube: Marble Arch
Barclays Cycle Hire: Park Lane, Hyde Park

The Animals in War Memorial can be found on PARK LANE at the end of Upper Brooke Street. Unveiled in 2004, the memorial remembers all animals that have been part of the British and Commonwealth armies throughout history.

The stunning Animals in War Memorial in the centre of Park Lane.

Although mechanisation of the British military was occurring in 1939, animals were still very much in use. Mules were used to transport stores to some of the more inhospitable fields of combat, with groups such as the Chindits using thousands of them. Pigeons were still widely employed to carry messages from the front line back to headquarters. Pigeon remains dating from the Second World War were found in a Surrey chimney in 2012 with a red canister attached to the bird's leg containing a coded message.

It was not only the British Army that used animals during the Second World War. Despite their blitzkrieg tactics, the bulk of the German Army was dependent on horse power to move its equipment.

Arthur 'Bomber' Harris Statue
STRAND

Tube: Temple
Barclays Cycle Hire: Strand, Strand

The memorial statue of Arthur 'Bomber' Harris is in front of St Clement Danes RAF church at the Fleet Street end of the STRAND and was unveiled by the Queen Mother in 1992.

As the Blitz wore on, and Great Britain stood alone, one of the few means of fighting back was with its bomber force. Harris became commander-in-chief of Bomber Command in February 1942, taking over one of the most potent weapons available to Britain at the time. A leader of men, Harris could be inflexible in his approach, but would make a decision and move on with his desire being to strengthen Bomber Command.

By the time Harris took over, Bomber Command tactics were beginning to change. The inability of crews to hit precise targets was being recognised and the idea of area bombing as an alternative tactic was being developed. Area bombing was, as the name implies, the targeting of a specific area, most notably towns and cities, and was a policy that was to be executed by Harris. Harris has often been vilified for this practice which, it was known, would likely result in many thousands of civilian deaths.

The belief was that the best way of destroying Germany's capacity for producing war materiel was by the total destruction of her industrial towns. Harris, writing after the war, was well aware that the policy of area bombing was thought to be entirely his and defended himself, pointing out that the decision was made by 'the Ministries, the Chiefs of Staff Committee, and by the War Cabinet'. The reality is, of course, that it was a combination of the two sides, with the War Cabinet supporting the policy and the Air Ministry removing any constraints on attacking cities, stating in a directive

The controversial figure of Arthur 'Bomber' Harris, commander of Britain's bomber force for much of the war.

that operations 'should now be focused on the morale of the enemy civil population and in particular, of industrial workers'. Harris undoubtedly believed that, at the time, area bombing was the best method of attack, and energetically carried out this policy. As a result, Harris will be remembered by many as a hero who struck a crucial blow to Nazi Germany and to others as a man responsible for countless, unnecessary, civilian deaths.

Australian War Memorial
WELLINGTON ARCH

Tube: Hyde Park Corner
Barclays Cycle Hire: Wellington Arch

The Australian War Memorial can be found near WELLINGTON ARCH on Hyde Park Corner. It is a semi-circular wall made from Australian granite and has the names of the 23,844 towns in which the Australian soldiers who died in both wars were born, along with the forty-seven battles in which they fought.

Australian forces fought in many of the most significant battles of the Second World War, either as part of the Commonwealth forces or as part of their own offensive against the Japanese. In the Pacific the Australians fought the Japanese, who had inflicted a series of catastrophic defeats in the region, culminating in the fall of Singapore. Australia herself was attacked for the first time in history when the Japanese bombed Darwin. The Australians, heavily

The magnificent Australian War Memorial is made from granite and engraved with the 23,844 home towns of the Australian soldiers who died in both wars.

involved in the counter-offensive, fought the Japanese until their eventual surrender in 1945.

The memorial was unveiled on 11 November 2003 by Queen Elizabeth II and is a permanent reminder of the 102,000 Australians who died during the First and Second World Wars.

Battle of Britain Monument
EMBANKMENT (NORTH SIDE)

Tube: Embankment
Barclays Cycle Hire: Embankment (Horse Guards), Westminster

The Battle of Britain Monument is a spectacular frieze full of evocative images alongside the names of the men and women who gave their lives in the battle fought over the skies of Britain between 10 July and 31 October 1940. It can be found on Victoria Embankment at the end of Richmond Terrace (which links Whitehall to the Embankment opposite Downing Street) and was unveiled on 18 September 2005, the sixty-fifth anniversary of the Battle of Britain.

The Battle of Britain Monument on the Embankment, commemorating all those who fought and died during Britain's darkest hour.

The Battle of Britain was a pivotal moment in the history of Britain and of the Second World War. Under orders from Hitler, Göring sent the Luftwaffe to wipe out the Royal Air Force – something that he boasted would be achieved 'in a matter of days'. These were desperate times for the British, with the RAF coming under constant attack.

There has been much speculation as to why the British won and how the Germans lost this aerial conflict. Tactically the British were very astute. Air Chief Marshal Hugh Dowding controlled his resources with aplomb, making the very best use of radar to try to ensure every raid was met. When they did meet in combat, both sides had their advantages. The aeroplanes were, in reality, a fairly even match: the Spitfire and Hurricane were excellent, but so was the Messerschmitt. The latter had one massive advantage, however, in that it had a 20mm cannon. The difference between the tiny 0.303 shells used by the British compared to the massive explosive cannon shells of the Messerschmitts is astounding. Luftwaffe planes were regularly able to return to their bases full of holes, but still operational.

On 7 September 1940, the Luftwaffe's primary tactics changed from targeting the RAF and their airfields to attacking London. Faulty German intelligence suggested the British were down to as few as 150 aircraft and, in part, it was hoped that such an attack would draw them out. While the RAF was in a precarious situation, it was not quite this dire. The start of the Blitz gave the RAF vital breathing space and allowed them to rebuild. On 15 September, heavy raids aimed at wiping out the remainder of the RAF were met with every aircraft available. The Luftwaffe were unable to recover from this onslaught and the heavy losses they suffered at the hands of an enemy they believed to be all but defeated. By the end of October the Battle of Britain was over, having been decisively won by the British.

The heroics of the RAF pilots (it should also never be forgotten that the British were augmented by Poles, French, Americans and pilots from many other nations) were immortalised by Churchill as 'the few' in his speech of 20 August 1940:

> The gratitude of every home in our Island, in our Empire, and indeed throughout the world, except in the abodes of the guilty, goes out to the British airmen who, undaunted by odds, unwearied in their constant challenge and mortal danger, are turning the tide of the World War by their prowess and by their devotion. Never in the field of human conflict was so much owed by so many to so few.

Bomber Command Memorial
GREEN PARK

Tube: Green Park
Barclays Cycle Hire: Green Park Station, West End

The memorial to the men of Bomber Command who lost their lives during the Second World War can be found towards the south-west corner of GREEN PARK. Depicting seven aircrew returning from a mission, it is sculpted in 9ft-high bronze and is covered by a roof made of aluminium reclaimed from a Handley Page Halifax III bomber shot down over Belgium in

One of London's newest memorials is dedicated to the men of Bomber Command, nearly half of whom lost their lives.

May 1944. The memorial is one of the most recent to be unveiled in London remembering the Second World War veterans and was opened by Queen Elizabeth II on 28 June 2012.

Bomber Command was established in 1936, and was led by the controversial Arthur 'Bomber' Harris from early 1942. The constant aerial threat posed by Bomber Command drew vital men, equipment and resources away from the German front-line forces and undeniably affected Germany's ability to fight. Bomber Command was responsible for one of the most impressive missions of the war, the Dam Busters raid, which destroyed dams around the Ruhr Valley. But, some of the activities of Bomber Command are steeped in controversy, such as the raid on Dresden in which 25,000 civilians lost their lives.

The men who flew in Bomber Command were among the bravest, knowing their odds of survival were poor. In all, 55,573 of the 125,000 men who served in it lost their lives and are worthy of the recognition this memorial brings. In December 2012 it was announced that the men of Bomber Command would be entitled to a clasp to be worn on their campaign medal as further recognition of their service during the war.

Canadian War Memorial
GREEN PARK

Tube: Green Park
Barclays Cycle Hire: Wellington Arch, Hyde Park

The Canadian War Memorial can be found near the Canada Gate entrance to GREEN PARK, close to Buckingham Palace. The memorial, unveiled by Queen Elizabeth II in 1994, is made of Canadian granite divided in two by a narrow walkway and is covered with bronze maple leaves.

Canadian forces were heavily engaged during the Second World War, their forces fighting alongside the British, American and those of other nations throughout Europe. Canadian soldiers landed alongside British commandos in the failed Dieppe raid – the only significant Allied attack on mainland France prior to the Normandy landings.

Canadian forces were again at the forefront of the assault on the Atlantic Wall on D-Day, when the 3rd Canadian Infantry Division landed on Juno beach. From this landing beach, Canadian soldiers fought to liberate Europe and defeat Nazi Germany, playing significant roles in the liberation of Belgium and the Netherlands.

The memorial pays tribute to the 1 million Canadian men and women who came to Britain to fight in both world wars and honours the 100,000 who were never to return.

The bronze maple leaves on the Canadian War Memorial in Green Park, which pays tribute to the 1 million Canadians who fought in both wars.

The Cenotaph
WHITEHALL

Tube: Embankment
Barclays Cycle Hire: Embankment (Horse Guards), Westminster

The Cenotaph can be found midway along WHITEHALL, in the centre of the road, and is close to Downing Street.

The Cenotaph, or empty tomb, was unveiled on 11 November 1920 and replaced the temporary structure which had been erected for the victory parade held in 1919 that came after the official end of the First World War. Since its unveiling, the Cenotaph has been Britain's official war memorial for all those who have lost their lives in conflicts around the world while in service to the country.

London's most iconic war memorial, the Cenotaph, dedicated to all those who have lost their lives while serving in Britain's armed forces.

After the conclusion of the Second World War, the dates of that war were added. Every year on Remembrance Sunday poppies are laid at the Cenotaph by members of the royal family, thus leading the Remembrance Day services in honour of all those who gave their lives.

Charles de Gaulle Statue
CARLTON GARDENS

See Free French HQ and Charles de Gaulle statue, p. 84.

Chindit Memorial
EMBANKMENT (NORTH SIDE)

Tube: Embankment
Barclays Cycle Hire: Embankment (Horse Guards), Westminster

The Chindit Memorial is situated behind the MoD main building, overlooking the Thames.

The Chindit Memorial is on a lawn in front of the MoD main building and overlooks the River Thames. It was unveiled on 16 October 1990 by HRH Prince Phillip, Duke of Edinburgh.

The Chindits were a force conceived by Orde Wingate to carry out long-range penetration behind Japanese lines in Burma. It was envisioned that the Chindits would operate in enemy territory for a significant period of time and would be supplied by air drops.

With General Wavell's support as commander-in-chief, Wingate got the necessary manpower to form this attacking force and, in June 1942, Wingate's ruthless training began, teaching the soldiers to accept the privations of the jungle. Kept on half rations, they carried out ferociously hard training almost from dawn to dusk, with forced marches, drills, bush craft, demolition training, as well as combat exercises. In February 1943, the first Chindit columns were marching into the jungle looking for the Japanese Army. Not all went to plan as mules misbehaved and men got lost, but notable successes ensued, such as the battle at Pinlebu where the railway line was cut in several places and two railway bridges were brought down.

The Second Chindit Expedition went ahead in 1944, starting with long marches into the formidable Burmese jungle that used mule trains to carry supplies to create strongholds complete with air landing strips. Wingate was thus able to fly between the strongholds to give orders and show his face, but it was one of these flights that cost him his life. While the cause has never been determined, what is known is that for some reason Wingate's plane crashed on the reverse side of a ridge, killing all on board.

This memorial is a fitting tribute to all the brave men who embarked on the Chindit expeditions into an unforgiving land to fight a ruthless enemy.

General Dwight D. Eisenhower Statue
GROSVENOR SQUARE

Tube: Bond Street
Barclays Cycle Hire: Grosvenor Square, Mayfair

The Eisenhower statue stands outside the front of the current US Embassy in GROSVENOR SQUARE and was unveiled in 1989. (See Eisenhower's HQ, p. 63.)

Eisenhower, commander-in-chief of the cross-Channel invasion force, who successfully led the Allied armies to victory over Nazi Germany.

The Gurkha Memorial Statue
HORSE GUARDS AVENUE

Tube: Embankment
Barclays Cycle Hire: Embankment (Horse Guards), Westminster

The Gurkha statue can be found opposite the main entrance of the Ministry of Defence building on HORSE GUARDS AVENUE, which runs between Whitehall and Victoria Embankment. The statue's plaque lists all the major campaigns

The Gurkha Memorial Statue outside the MoD main building immortalises some of the finest soldiers ever to fight with the British Army.

the Gurkhas fought in during the Second World War, including Burma, North Africa, Iraq, Syria, Greece and Italy, to name but a few.

Up until the outbreak of the Second World War there were around twenty Gurkha battalions within the British Army; however, after the BEF's evacuation from Dunkirk the Nepalese government offered to increase recruitment to raise this number to thirty-five battalions. Astonishingly, the Nepalese actually created forty-five Gurkha battalions, with a wartime peak of a phenomenal 112,000 men.

The Gurkhas predominantly fought the Japanese throughout Burma under General Slim during the Second World War, building on their already fearsome reputation. Such was Slim's admiration of the Gurkhas' skill in combat that in his book, *Defeat to Victory*, he details a single minor action he witnessed by a platoon of Gurkhas taking a Japanese defensive position. The eleven Victoria Crosses won by Gurkhas during the war give some indication of what the Japanese were up against.

Holocaust Memorial Garden
HYDE PARK

Tube: Knightsbridge
Barclays Cycle Hire: Albert Gate, Knightsbridge

The Holocaust Memorial Garden can be found in an area of HYDE PARK known as the Dell, to the east of the bottom corner of the Serpentine. It consists of several large stones with inscriptions set in a small garden area.

The Holocaust Memorial was unveiled in the 1980s and is one of many around the world that remembers the 6 million Jews, and other peoples, murdered by the Nazis.

The Holocaust Memorial Day is held every year on 27 January, the date on which Auschwitz was liberated by Soviet forces.

Eagle Squadrons Memorial
GROSVENOR SQUARE

Tube: Bond Street
Barclays Cycle Hire: Grosvenor Square, Mayfair

The Eagle Squadrons Memorial can be found in Grosvenor Square Gardens opposite the Roosevelt Memorial and was unveiled in May 1986.

At the outbreak of war America did not officially take sides, but some young Americans, either through ideology or just seeking adventure, ignored this and came to Britain to fight the Luftwaffe.

The first American to arrive and join the RAF was Billy Fiske, who had won two gold medals for bobsledding.

The Eagle Squadrons who fought in the Battle of Britain were made up of American pilots who volunteered against their country's wishes. Their memorial can be found in Grosvenor Square.

To do this he risked his citizenship, for US law stated it was illegal to join a warring power's military service, punishment for which was imprisonment, a $10,000 fine and loss of US citizenship. He served from September 1939 to August 1940, when he died from the severe burns he received when his plane was hit. His heroism led to a funeral service at St Paul's, attended by many of his fellow countrymen who, like Fiske, had managed to avoid the FBI agents to arrive in Britain to fight.

There were so many young Americans heading for Britain that Eagle squadrons were formed. The idea of an all-American fighter squadron was encouraged by Churchill and by the time America officially joined the conflict 244 men had flown in defence of Great Britain. Once trained, the men of the Eagle squadrons were thrown into the fray, shooting down more than seventy German planes. But this did come at a cost, with over 40 per cent of the Eagles being killed in action.

The memorial celebrates and remembers their heroism and courage, fighting and dying for a cause that was not, at that time, seen by many to be theirs.

Franklin D. Roosevelt Statue
GROSVENOR SQUARE

Tube: Bond Street
Barclays Cycle Hire: Grosvenor Square, Mayfair

The Roosevelt statue can be found in Grosvenor Square Gardens and was unveiled by Eleanor Roosevelt on 12 April 1948.

Franklin D. Roosevelt was elected as President of the United States of America in November 1932, the first of his four terms in office, during which he watched Europe edge ever closer to conflict. America became more divided as to what her involvement should be; there were many supporters who felt America would have to enter the conflict at some stage and believed the sooner they did this the easier it would be. However, there was a very strong group who believed that America should, at all costs, avoid entering the war.

It was with this background that Roosevelt found himself; to enter the conflict could have jeopardised his position – something that could have been fatal for Britain if an isolationist had got into office – but to do nothing could well have left the Nazis as masters of all Europe. Roosevelt clearly wanted, as any sensible person would, to avoid entering the war, but equally felt compelled to provide assistance.

Franklin D. Roosevelt, the president who oversaw America's entry into the war. He died just a few months before victory over Japan.

One of the first tangible signs that America was creeping away from her neutral position was with the initiation of the Lend-Lease programme in 1941. After a slow start, Lend-Lease allowed significant resources to enter Britain. The next step up was the dispatch of 4,000 marines to Iceland, to take over its defence from the British. They also extended the US naval protection zone to Iceland, although this only covered the defence of American ships to that point.

Roosevelt continued to reassure the British with comments suggesting that America would enter the war while often publically saying the opposite in his own country. It is not clear whether or not Roosevelt would have committed American forces to support Britain without the intervention of Japan. Immediately after the Japanese attacked Pearl Harbor, America declared war on Japan and then, shortly after, Germany declared war on America. These two acts did much to save Britain, as Churchill well knew. He euphorically received the news at Chequers of the Japanese attack and declared war on them immediately.

The American president called Churchill and simply said, 'we are in the same boat now'. Once in the war, Roosevelt, without question, dedicated all his country's resources to winning that conflict and by spring 1942 American troops started arriving in Britain in large numbers. While not without its occasional difficulties, the relationship flourished. Roosevelt was present at all the major negotiations and forged the path ahead with Britain and the Soviet Union.

Roosevelt died from a cerebral haemorrhage on 12 April 1945 and was replaced by Truman. While he did not live to see the eventual surrender of Germany and Japan, which were only a few weeks and months away, he would have known victory was a certainty thanks, in no small part, to his leadership.

George VI Statue

CARLTON HOUSE TERRACE

Tube: Charing Cross
Barclays Cycle Hire: Waterloo Place, St James's

The statue of King George VI is located at the end of CARLTON HOUSE TERRACE, overlooking the Mall and St James's Park. It has since been adapted from its original design to include a statue of Elizabeth, the Queen Mother, and a frieze commemorating the royal couple's achievements throughout their lives.

King George VI will always be remembered as a reluctant king due to his unexpected ascension to the throne in December 1936, when his elder brother, Edward VIII, abdicated. The then Duke of York had always looked up to his elder brother and was appalled by the thought of becoming king. Despite this, King George VI took up his duties without complaint at a time when Britain and the world were about to be thrust into the most turbulent upheaval that was the Second World War.

The new king had much to learn, but took to his role with a clear devotion to do his best for the country. The first real event of note that he had to negotiate was the Munich Agreement signed by Chamberlain in September 1938. The king had little, if anything, to do with the discussions led by Chamberlain in Munich. When Chamberlain came back with his 'scrap of paper' claiming to have secured 'peace in our time', the king, like so many others, wanted to

One of the impressive friezes surrounding the King George VI statue on the Mall.

believe he had achieved just that. Having appeared on the balcony of the palace with Chamberlain to celebrate the achievement – a break in protocol – the king was somewhat taken aback by the anti-Munich feelings and the criticism he faced for his apparent endorsement of the policy.

The king made continued efforts to improve Britain's standing with other countries and his visit to Canada and America in May and June 1939 did much to improve Anglo-American relations. The king and queen stayed for a few days at Roosevelt's Hyde Park Estate and family home, where Roosevelt made a strong impression on the king.

The king still had problems with Chamberlain's government in that important matters were not brought to his attention until after the event, such as the public assurance that Britain would uphold the 'Polish Guarantee'. A week later Britain was at war with Germany and nine months later Chamberlain, proven to be out of his depth directing the war effort, had been replaced by Churchill.

George, somewhat surprised by Churchill's appointment as prime minister over Lord Halifax, did get one thing he had been pressing for: a National government. This was to take in politicians from all sides in a joint effort to steer the country through the crisis. The king's relationship with Churchill soon flourished at their weekly lunch meetings where they discussed, alone and with complete openness, the conduct of the war.

The king at this time also proved himself capable of understanding the plight of the people in Britain. He at no point would entertain the idea of leaving the country, and remained in London with the queen for the majority of the war in a partly mothballed Buckingham Palace. George VI did all he could to improve and bolster the British morale with countless visits to bomb-damaged towns and cities. The perception of a monarch removed from his subjects was thus broken down and the resolve of the people of Britain to fight on was hardened.

One of his later tasks of the war was to persuade Churchill from heading out on the ships bombarding the French coast on D-Day. While the king had been eager to head out with Churchill, he swiftly reconsidered when his Private Secretary asked him to advise Princess Elizabeth as to who should be the next prime minister should both he and Churchill be killed. The king then spent some time convincing Churchill not to depart aboard HMS *Belfast* – something he finally acquiesced to, albeit a little reluctantly. Ten days after D-Day George was stood on the Normandy beaches watching the beginning of the end of Hitler's reign.

While it can never be known how Edward would have fared as king during the upheaval of the Second World War, without a doubt King George VI proved himself to be a great monarch who helped guide the country from near defeat to ultimate victory.

Air Chief Marshal Hugh Dowding Statue
STRAND

Tube: Temple
Barclays Cycle Hire: Strand, Strand

The memorial statue of Air Chief Marshal Hugh Dowding is in front of St Clement Danes RAF church, which is at the Fleet Street end of the STRAND.

Air Chief Marshal Hugh Dowding, born in Scotland in 1882, briefly flew in the First World War. In the early 1930s he was responsible for much of the research and development within the RAF and oversaw the introduction of both the Hurricane and the Spitfire into service. Come 1936 he was appointed as commander-in-chief of Fighter Command and was directly responsible for Britain's fighter force, which was to prove so decisive in those months after the disaster in France.

Dowding was prepared to take on new ideas and to change anything that did not work. Despite being seen as a rather 'stiff' individual, he was to prove more than equal to the task ahead. He had appreciated, throughout the campaign in France, the simple risk of hurling more of his precious aircraft into a doomed venture. Every fighter destroyed in France meant there was one less to defend the homeland and, with numbers being so tight, he knew that a few aircraft could mean the difference between survival and destruction. While he continually opposed the sending of aircraft to France, he was at times compelled to, and as a result only had at his disposal 504 Hurricanes and Spitfires with which to fight the upcoming Battle of Britain.

Air Chief Marshal Hugh Dowding, whose tactical brilliance helped win the Battle of Britain.

During the phoney war, Dowding made many changes to the defence system around Britain. At the heart of this was the radar early warning system, as well as the massive Royal Observer Corps. Dowding's defensive system relied on a clear standardised approach to the work that they were to undertake. Information was sent in by the observers and radar stations; it was then filtered and resources were used as deemed best by Fighter Command. However, he ensured that Fighter Command was able to use its meagre resources to the best possible effect, and by the end of October 1940 the Battle of Britain was over.

Field Marshal Jan Christian Smuts Statue
PARLIAMENT SQUARE

Tube: Westminster
Barclays Cycle Hire: Embankment (Horse Guards), Westminster

Jan Christian Smuts was the Prime Minster of South Africa during the Second World War and a close friend of Churchill, much evidenced by the correspondence between the two. Smuts was to be awarded the rank of field marshal in the British Army, the first South African to be so honoured.

London Firefighters Memorial
ST PAUL'S CHURCHYARD

Tube: St Paul's
Barclays Cycle Hire: Godliman Street, St Paul's

The Firefighters Memorial is fittingly situated in front of St Paul's Cathedral, where some of the fiercest fires were fought, and was unveiled by the Queen Mother in 1991.

The bravery of these men and women was without question as they went out night after night to bring under control the fires started by Luftwaffe bombing in London, Coventry, Bristol and scores of other cities across the country.

In total, 1,027 men and women of the fire service died as a direct result of enemy action during the war. A service of remembrance is held on the second Sunday of September every year.

The firefighters statue in St Paul's Churchyard is dedicated to all those who battled the infernos caused by German bombing.

Field Marshal Montgomery Statue
WHITEHALL

Tube: Embankment
Barclays Cycle Hire: Embankment (Horse Guards), Westminster

Montgomery was a career soldier who joined the Army straight from school and went on to serve in France in the First World War, where he won a DSO. From the chaos of that war, Montgomery set about climbing the ranks in the regular army, with postings to a variety of places, including Egypt. It was six years before he returned to England as a brigadier to command the 9th Infantry Division in Portsmouth. From here he returned to Palestine, coming back to England shortly before the war started.

Britain was already at war with Germany when he was given command of the 3rd Division in France, after much persistence, where he was able to put into practice his theories on modern soldiering.

Those first weeks of fighting that followed the phoney war showed much of Montgomery's skill as a commander. His division advanced into Belgium to meet the German onslaught and carried out a complex reorganisation to plug the gap left by the Belgian Army when they capitulated. However, it was a defeat, and Montgomery, now in command of II Corps, headed back to Britain via Dunkirk.

It was due to the tragic death of General Gott that Montgomery was given his most famous command: the Eighth Army. Having received his appointment, Gott's aircraft was shot down and Montgomery was hurriedly redirected to Cairo. He soon defeated Rommel at the Battle of El Alamein, which was possibly the highlight of his career, for he took the name 'Montgomery of Alamein' after that victory.

It was with this success and lessons learnt that Montgomery embarked on the cross-Channel invasion under Eisenhower, commanding 21st Army Group. Montgomery was instrumental in the planning of the D-Day operations, but his performance has been criticised, mainly for the apparent lack of drive in taking Caen. However bitter the fighting around Caen was, the town itself was not the objective; that was to suck in the German forces to ensure that the American breakout on the western flank would be decisive.

Montgomery had one final plan to bring about a quick and conclusive end to the war known as Operation Market Garden. Approved by Eisenhower, Montgomery's plan involved dropping thousands of men throughout the Netherlands to capture key bridges, culminating in the bridge at Arnhem, with an armoured thrust racing to relieve these airborne forces. This, however, was one battle that could not be claimed as a success. The airborne forces were dispatched, but the armoured column was unable to make it to Arnhem and the stranded British troops rapidly began to lose the war of attrition. The troops were eventually withdrawn and the offensive across Europe continued on the broad front

The statue of Montgomery, Britain's most famous battlefield commander of the Second World War.

favoured by Eisenhower rather than the concentrated thrust Montgomery had desired.

The field marshal was to have the final say in northern Europe when he took the surrender of the German forces in Holland, north-west Germany and Denmark from General Admiral von Friedeburg, General Kinzel, Rear Admiral Wagner and Major Freidel on 4 May 1945.

Montgomery returned to England a national hero and was elevated to the highest position in the British Army: Chief of the Imperial General Staff (CIGS). He was also given a peerage, taking the title Viscount Montgomery of Alamein. Montgomery died in March 1976.

Lord Mountbatten Statue
HORSE GUARDS ROAD

Tube: Embankment
Barclays Cycle Hire: Embankment (Horse Guards), Westminster

The statue of Lord Mountbatten can be found overlooking Horse Guards parade from the green to the rear of the Foreign and Commonwealth Office. (See 15 Chester Street, p. 32).

Lord Louis Mountbatten, who rose to command all Allied forces in South East Asia.

Norwegian-British Friendship Memorial
HYDE PARK

Tube: Marble Arch
Barclays Cycle Hire: Cumberland Gate, Hyde Park

The Norwegian-British Friendship Memorial can be found in HYDE PARK and was erected by the Royal Norwegian Navy and Merchant fleet in 1978 to thank the British people for providing a safe haven throughout the war.

Lord Portal of Hungerford Statue
EMBANKMENT (NORTH SIDE)

Tube: Embankment
Barclays Cycle Hire: Embankment (Horse Guards), Westminster

The statue of Lord Portal of Hungerford can be found in front of the MoD main building, on the EMBANKMENT side overlooking the Thames.

Lord Portal of Hungerford took over as commander-in-chief of Bomber Command when Ludlow-Hewitt left in April 1940. By October 1940 he had moved again, this time being appointed as Chief of the Air Staff with the rank of air chief marshal.

After the war he went on to work at a high level in Britain's atomic programme as Controller of Production (Atomic Energy). He died 22 April 1971.

Lord Portal of Hungerford, Chief of the Air Staff from October 1940.

RAF Memorial
EMBANKMENT (NORTH SIDE)

Tube: Embankment
Barclays Cycle Hire: Embankment (Horse Guards), Westminster

The RAF Memorial can be found on the banks of the River Thames in front of the MoD main building, with a striking gilded eagle perched on its peak looking south towards France.

Built by the RAF to commemorate the brave officers and men who flew in the First World War, it now is a permanent reminder to all those men and women who have given their lives in the service of the RAF throughout its history.

Royal Navy Air Service & Fleet Air Arm Memorial
EMBANKMENT (NORTH SIDE)

Tube: Embankment
Barclays Cycle Hire: Embankment (Horse Guards), Westminster

The Royal Navy Air Service & Fleet Air Arm Memorial can be found in front of the MoD main building and remembers those who served in those branches of the navy who operated planes from RN ships during the Second World War.

The Royal Navy Air Service & Fleet Air Arm memorial is on the lawn outside MoD Main Building.

Royal Tank Regiment Memorial
WHITEHALL COURT

Tube: Embankment
Barclays Cycle Hire: Whitehall Place, Strand

The Royal Tank Regiment Memorial can be found on the corner of WHITEHALL COURT and Whitehall Place, and is opposite the Corinthia Hotel (which was known as the Metropole Building during the war). It was unveiled by Queen Elizabeth II, colonel-in-chief of the Tank Regiment, on 13 June 2006 and depicts the five-man crew of a Second World War-era Comet tank.

Tanks were first used during the Great War, where they helped to break the stalemate of the trench warfare being able to advance on the opposition trenches, impervious to their machine guns.

The Second World War brought the tank to the fore as a major offensive weapon, with great tank battles being fought. The German advances though Poland and France were led by Heinz Guderian who early on had realised the offensive capability of the tank, or 'striking power' as he described it: the measure of your ability to attack your opponent's defences.

The Tank Corps became the Royal Tank Regiment (RTR) in 1939 and was immediately up against Guderian's Panzer divisions. The RTR acquitted themselves well, but were, as much as anything, undone by the inability to replace their losses, which the Germans had prepared for. One account of the RTR's success was when two Matilda Mk 2 tanks, commanded by Major King and Sergeant Doyle, romped through German lines, taking on all whom they encountered. German 3.7mm anti-tank guns were unable to penetrate the armour and were run over, while retreating soldiers provided ample targets

The Royal Tank Regiment memorial outside the old War Office building.

for the tanks' machine guns. They then took on and destroyed numerous German tanks until they eventually were obliged to surrender.

The RTR was very much at the fore of the action for the rest of the war, taking part in the spectacular tank battles in the desert against Rommel. They were again in action on D-Day as they landed to support the forward troops, often in the 'Hobart Funnies' – a range of tanks that had been modified to fulfil specific tasks. The Funnies carried demolition charges, were able to 'swim', could clear paths through minefields and build bridges.

General Sikorski Statue
PORTLAND PLACE

See Polish Government in Exile and Sikorski Statue, p. 53.

Special Operations Executive Memorial
EMBANKMENT (SOUTH SIDE)

Tube: Lambeth North
Barclays Cycle Hire: Fire Brigade Pier, Vauxhall

The SOE Memorial is off Lambeth Palace Road, near Lambeth Bridge and Lambeth Palace, and overlooks the River Thames. The memorial remembers the sacrifice made by all the agents of SOE who operated in enemy-occupied territories, with only torture and death the likely outcome if captured. It consists of a bust of Violette Szabo (see p. 157), who lived in the Lambeth area before joining SOE.

Field Marshal William Slim Statue
WHITEHALL

Tube: Embankment
Barclays Cycle Hire: Embankment (Horse Guards), Westminster

The statue of Field Marshal William Joseph Slim, 1st Viscount Slim KG, GCB, GCMG, GCVO, GBE, DSO, MC, KStJ can be found on Raleigh Green to the left of Alanbrooke and Montgomery. Raleigh Green is located on WHITEHALL to the side of the MoD main building.

Slim was a career soldier, but it was not until midway through the Second World War that his true skill as a military tactician came to light, when,

'Bill' Slim, one of Britain's finest wartime commanders. He turned the defeat by the Japanese in Burma into victory.

in 1942, he was promoted to lieutenant general and appointed commander of the I Burma Corps.

The British forces in Burma had no plan as to what they would actually do if Burma was invaded and as a result were steadily driven back by the Japanese onslaught. In the chaos and retreat, Slim was put in command of the now disintegrating Burma corps. He successfully, in the most dreadful conditions and against the odds, managed to extract a large portion of its men, albeit with little or no equipment, back to India.

Out of the remnants of this defeat, the Fourteenth Army was formed. Having witnessed the previous failures, Slim set about creating an army capable of taking on the Japanese. The greatest challenge Slim foresaw was ensuring his men used the jungle and did not see it as an impassable obstacle. The Japanese Army regularly took long detours through the jungle to outflank the retreating British forces and attack them. This was a tactic Slim's men were to emulate upon their advance through Burma to Rangoon.

Slim's Fourteenth Army repeatedly beat back the Japanese forces until they were routed, often with meagre supplies and second-rate equipment. The Fourteenth Army dubbed itself 'the forgotten army' due to this lack of equipment and an apparent indifference to their campaign back home.

The Fourteenth Army's campaign ended with the Japanese surrender after the atomic bombing of Hiroshima and Nagasaki. Slim went on to many other varied appointments including Governor of Australia. He died 14 December 1970.

Winston Churchill Statue
PARLIAMENT SQUARE

Tube: Westminster
Barclays Cycle Hire: Embankment (Horse Guards), Westminster

The statue of Churchill, the most famous British figure to come out of the Second World War, who died on 24 January 1965, is on the south-east corner of PARLIAMENT SQUARE.

Churchill rose to the highest office from what he described as his 'wilderness years', during which he held no political office and thought his return to the front benches unlikely. Famous for his vocal anti-appeasement stance, Churchill did not endear himself to his colleagues but, as time wore on, his view on rearmament began to look like a missed opportunity.

Churchill seemed to take it as his responsibility to harangue Chamberlain at every opportunity, as war drew closer, on any and all matters he thought vital to the defence of the country. Once given charge of the Admiralty and a place in the Cabinet his influence grew and gradually he began taking a more and more prominent role.

By the time Chamberlain stepped down, it was thought to be between Churchill and Halifax as to who would become the new premier. In the event, Halifax withdrew and Churchill became prime minister, which was something very few would have thought possible twelve months previously.

From this point on, Churchill strove with single-mindedness to win the war. While his war diaries give some interesting insights into how he perceived the desperate situation Britain was in, he never wavered in his belief in certain victory. While he could interfere on an operational level and insist on pet projects being pushed through, despite advice from others, Churchill was absolute in his determination to crush the Nazis.

With victory announced, Churchill addressed the crowds gathered on Whitehall and told them: 'this is your victory.' With one voice they shouted back: 'no, it's yours.' A fitting accolade to Churchill, Britain's greatest war leader.

Churchill overlooking Parliament Square and the Houses of Parliament.

Monument to the Women of World War II
WHITEHALL

Tube: Embankment
Barclays Cycle Hire: Embankment (Horse Guards), Westminster

The Monument to the Women of World War II can be found midway along WHITEHALL, in the centre of the road next to the Cenotaph, close to Downing Street. The memorial celebrates the role women played, and those who lost their lives, during the Second World War. It was unveiled by Queen Elizabeth II in July 2005.

At the onset of the Second World War, many jobs were effectively closed to women, but as men left to take up front-line roles in the armed forces, a critical need to fill those vacated positions arose. Women across the nation took up employment in every job imaginable, from driving buses and trains to manufacturing the arms and armaments needed to fight the war.

The First Aid Nursing Yeomanry (FANY) was also created and young women began taking up direct military roles, such as driving staff cars and crewing the anti-aircraft guns defending the country. A great number of women worked in the RAF plotting rooms tracking enemy aircraft, while others flew transport aircraft around Britain. By the end of the war a significant part of the huge staff at Bletchley Park were women, who were part of the team that was regularly breaking the critical German Enigma codes.

The Women's Voluntary Service (WVS) was formed by Lady Reading on a request from the Home Office in 1938. The WVS carried out remarkable and selfless work helping with the evacuation of children, the running of mobile canteens and finding housing for people that had been bombed out.

The Women of World War II memorial on Whitehall remembers the many sacrifices made by the women of Great Britain during the war and the part they played in bringing about victory.

Britain has a wealth of military history associated with it, with thousands of battles having being fought in its name across the globe. Many of the deeds of the men and women who fought for Britain throughout the years have been immortalised in memorials covering centuries of conflict.

Such a rich military history is evident in London through the very buildings that make up the city, such as the Admiralty building, the War Office and the War Rooms. The Foot Guards and Life Guards who can be seen on duty around the royal palaces are a constant visual reminder of the country's military heritage.

Whilst in London, there are many opportunities for a visitor to learn more about Britain, and London's, military past at a variety of museums. The London Transport Museum offers a fascinating insight into life in London during the Blitz and how the Underground network was used to shelter hundreds of thousands of people every night. The National Army Museum offers an unparalleled insight into the role of the British Army, while the Guards and Household Cavalry museums take the visitor through the history of those individual regiments from their formation to the present day.

London Transport Museum
COVENT GARDEN PIAZZA

Tube: Covent Garden
Barclays Cycle Hire: Tavistock Street, Covent Garden

The entrance to the London Transport Museum can be found on the corner of the COVENT GARDEN PIAZZA. The museum is an excellent central London attraction that surprises in its sheer entertainment value. There is a historic collection of transport on display including buses, Underground trains and carriages. There are many from the wartime period, some of which visitors can climb aboard.

One of the most interesting aspects of the museum is the Underground posters, all as distinctive as they are different. There are many from the war period and beyond, such as the one encouraging Londoners to be patient while the bomb damage backlog was cleared after the war.

The Underground at war is marked by a curious one-person shelter: a metal cone that the 'last man' could sit in during a bombing raid. There are enlightening stories and memorabilia from both wars along with a film

The entrance to the London Transport Museum is found in the corner of the Covent Garden piazza.

showing how London Transport kept its services running. It also shows what happened behind the scenes to keep those sheltering on the Underground as comfortable as possible.

The museum is aimed at keeping children entertained as much as it informs the adults, with many interactive displays, including Tube train driving which will keep everyone occupied for hours.

The shop is also well stocked with quirky London Transport souvenirs, from the ubiquitous museum shop tea towels and pencils to uniquely brilliant London Transport-themed luggage and furniture. Via the online shop it is possible to browse the huge collection of London Underground posters as well as order prints in various sizes and finishes. There are also occasional opportunities to purchase reclaimed fittings such as luggage racks from 1960s Underground trains.

General Admission Information

Website: www.ltmuseum.co.uk
Telephone: 020 7379 6344
Admission Costs: Adult: £15.00
                   Child: £11.50
                   Concessions: £11.50

National Army Museum
ROYAL HOSPITAL ROAD

Tube: Sloane Square
Barclays Cycle Hire: Flood Street, Chelsea

The National Army Museum is dedicated to preserving the history of the British Army and 'connecting the British public with its Army'. It is found on ROYAL HOSPITAL ROAD, next door to the Royal Hospital Chelsea.

The museum explores the role of the Army as Britain extended its reach across the globe through colonial expansion. The Army was to play a vital role in protecting trade routes and extending the borders of the British empire from America to Australia, fighting around the world to protect Britain's interests.

Come the twentieth century, Britain found itself deeply and bitterly locked in two world wars that were to shape the future of Europe and the world. The involvement of the British Army throughout these conflicts, and the part they played in the ultimate victory in 1945, are showcased.

The British Army has played a substantial part in British, and indeed world, history, which the National Army Museum allows the visitor to explore. The museum is clear that its aim is to allow the visitor to see the facts presented and allows them to make up their own mind about the actions of the British Army throughout history.

General Admission Information
Website: www.nam.ac.uk
Telephone: 020 7881 6606
Admission Costs: Free for all

Imperial War Museum
LAMBETH ROAD

Tube: Lambeth North
Barclays Cycle Hire: Kennington Road, Vauxhall

No visit to London would be complete without going to the Imperial War Museum. It has a breathtaking array of collections and artefacts from both world wars and every conflict in between and after. It is very easy to find, with the massive naval guns at the entrance, and is only a short walk from Lambeth North Underground station.

The Imperial War Museum was set up during the last years of the Great War in 1917, ostensibly to display all material of interest relating to that war. It was given the title 'Imperial War Museum', with an Act of Parliament formally establishing the museum in 1920. The original museum was located in Crystal Palace, but in 1936 it moved to its current home in Lambeth and the site of the Bethlem Royal Hospital, more commonly known as Bedlam.

The museum closed for the duration of the Second World War and as many of its collections as possible were moved to safety. The museum was to find itself on the front line when a bomb damaged the naval galleries, destroying a Short seaplane.

The Imperial War Museum collections now cover any conflict that the armed forces have taken part in since 1914. The museum is also responsible for the upkeep of HMS *Belfast* and the Churchill War Rooms. The museum has further sites at Duxford and Manchester.

General Admission Information
Website: www.iwm.org.uk
Telephone: 020 7416 5000
Admission Costs: Free for all

Churchill War Rooms
CLIVE STEPS, KING CHARLES STREET

Tube: Westminster
Barclays Cycle Hire: Embankment (Horse Guards), Westminster

For a real, and almost unparalleled, insight into what life was like during the Second World War, a visit to the Churchill War Rooms is essential. Located in the heart of Whitehall with a small, but very obvious, entrance overlooking St James's Park, it is easily accessible and should not be missed (see War Rooms, Whitehall, p. 105)

The War Rooms were locked up as soon as the Japanese surrender was taken in 1945 and were left virtually untouched for several decades afterwards. While an Act of Parliament sought to preserve the rooms as a historic site, access and even knowledge of it remained highly restricted until the 1970s, when the Imperial War Museum was given the task of preserving them. The main rooms were opened in 1984, with additional areas being opened in 2003. A museum dedicated to Winston Churchill has also been added in more recent years.

General Admission Information
Website: www.iwm.org.uk/visits/churchill-war-rooms
Telephone: 020 7930 6961
Admission Costs: Adult: £17
                          Child: Free
                          Concessions: £13.60

HMS *Belfast*
THE QUEEN'S WALK

Tube: London Bridge
Barclays Cycle Hire: Tooley Street, Bermondsey

HMS *Belfast* is moored in the Thames opposite the Tower of London. Access to the ship is via a jetty on the south side of the river just along from Tower Bridge. If you have ever wondered what life might be like in the Royal Navy then a visit to HMS *Belfast* will enlighten you.

HMS *Belfast* was built in 1936, launched in 1938 and was fully commissioned in 1939, just in time for the outbreak of war. However, the largest and most powerful cruiser of the Royal Navy had a somewhat unlucky entrance to the conflict, hitting a magnetic mine after only two months at

HMS *Belfast*, an impressive sight even today, moored on the Thames.

sea, which put her out of action for three years. On re-joining the fleet in 1942 she spent much of her time protecting the Arctic convoys taking vital supplies to Russia and played a part in the Battle of North Cape during which the *Scharnhorst* was sunk.

After the Second World War, HMS *Belfast* was involved in the Korean conflict supporting British and American troops, and then went on to carry out peacekeeping duties until she was retired from service in 1963. The ship was acquired by the Imperial War Museum and was opened to the public on Trafalgar Day, 21 October, 1971.

HMS *Belfast* is a fantastically preserved ship and is a memorial to the men who served on her, and in the Royal Navy, as well as being a historical artefact. HMS *Belfast* is a great day out for adults and especially children, who will love being able to climb around a real war ship, making the experience something of an adventure.

General Admission Information

Website: www.iwm.org.uk/visits/hms-belfast
Telephone: 020 7940 6300
Admission Costs: Adult: £14.50
                   Child: Free
                   Concessions: £11.60

The Guards Museum
WELLINGTON BARRACKS, BIRDCAGE WALK

Tube: St James's Park
Barclays Cycle Hire: Butler Place, Westminster

The Guards Museum can be found on BIRDCAGE WALK, between Wellington Barracks and the Guards Chapel, moments away from Buckingham Palace. Go in through the gate and head down the steps between the two sentry boxes to your right.

Along with the two divisions of Household Cavalry, the Guards divisions make up Her Majesty's Household Division, members of which can be seen on guard at the royal palaces. The Guards Museum is dedicated to the history of the five regiments of Foot Guards formed by the Grenadier, Coldstream, Scots, Irish and Welsh Guards.

If you want to find out more about the history of the Guards and the role they play in the armed forces outside of the ceremonial duties for which they are famed, then this excellent museum is the place to go.

If you want a photograph next to one of the Guards, then head towards the entrance to St James's Palace at the bottom on St James's Street, where it joins Pall Mall. There are nearly always guardsmen on duty, but without the thronging masses experienced in Horse Guards trying to get a photograph with members of the Household Cavalry.

General Admission Information
Website: www.theguardsmuseum.com
Telephone: 020 7414 3271
Admission Costs: Adult: £5
                  Child: Free
                  Concessions: £2.50

The Household Cavalry Museum
HORSE GUARDS, WHITEHALL

Tube: Westminster
Barclays Cycle Hire: Embankment (Horse Guards), Westminster

The entrance to the Household Cavalry Museum can be found directly off Horse Guards Parade. If you are walking down WHITEHALL you will not be able to miss the Household Cavalry soldiers on horseback at the entrance to the parade ground, complete with signs warning the tourists that the horses 'might bite'.

The Household Cavalry make up the Household Division along with the Foot Guards and are known throughout the world for their guard and ceremonial duties, but it is a mistake to think that is all the most senior regiment of the British Army does.

In 1939, the Household Cavalry consisted of the Life Guards, the Royal Horse Guards and the Royal Dragoons (the Royal Horse Guards (Blues) and the Royal Dragoons were merged in 1969 to become the Blues and Royals). The Life Guards contributed men to both Household Cavalry regiments during the war. They were present at the D-Day landings in Normandy and were at the spearhead of the Guards Armoured Divisions, which liberated Brussels. Similarly, the Blues also contributed men to both 1st and 2nd Household Calvary Regiments seeing action in Palestine, Syria and Normandy before entering the German naval base of Cuxhaven in 1945.

General Admission Information

Website: www.householdcavalrymuseum.co.uk
Telephone: 020 7930 3070
Admission Costs: Adult: £6
                    Child: £4
                    Concessions: £4

The Fusilier Museum
TOWER OF LONDON

Tube: Tower Hill
Barclays Cycle Hire: Tower Gardens, Tower

The Fusilier Museum is located within the TOWER OF LONDON and aims to 'preserve the memory and related heritage of the Royal Fusiliers and from 1968 the Royal Regiment of Fusiliers'. The museum contains an entire history of the fusiliers from their early days to the present.

General Admission Information

Website: www.fusiliermuseumlondon.org
Telephone: 020 3166 9612
Admission Costs: Free with entry to the Tower of London

Firepower, Royal Artillery Museum
ROYAL ARSENAL, WOOLWICH

Docklands Light Railway: Woolwich Arsenal
Barclays Cycle Hire: None close

The Royal Artillery Museum moved to the ROYAL ARSENAL in 2001, when it also took its current name 'Firepower'.

Artillery has been used, since the inception of the early cannon, in every major conflict throughout the world. Artillery has formed the backbone of modern armies as a vital tool to launch projectiles at distant enemy targets.

The First World War saw savage bombardments of enemy lines by massed artillery pieces, which were the main offensive weapon of both sides. Come the Second World War, that situation had changed with the advent of air power and advances in tank design, both of which brought about changes to the formation of the Royal Artillery Regiment.

Not only were the Royal Artillery responsible for manning their guns to take on the enemy at range, but they were also responsible for air defences and anti-tank weapons. Artillery was also at the core of many major offensives, with Montgomery using massive artillery bombardments to precede his offensive at El Alamein and the crossing of the Rhine.

The museum gives a captivating insight into 700 years of world artillery history and has much to offer adults and children alike, such as the 'ground shaking Field of Fire audio-visual show' which 'puts you in the midst of battle'.

General Admission Information
Website: www.firepower.org.uk
Telephone: 020 8855 7755
Admission Costs: Adult: £5.30
                 Child: £2.50
                 Concessions: £4.60

Other Museums
There are a whole range of other much smaller museums dotted around London that offer insights into specific regiments or military subjects, such as the Museum of British Military Music, which can be found in Twickenham. Many buildings with military collections will allow the public to visit for guided tours, but are often by appointment only, such as the Royal Hospital (home of the Chelsea Pensioners), the London Scottish Regiment Museum and the

The Royal Artillery in action during the Normandy Campaign, 1944.

London Irish Rifles Museum. As such, it is best to check first before visiting. A more detailed list of London's military museums, with contact details, can be found at www.armymuseums.org.uk.

Other museums and buildings that can be visited, which have a link to the Second World War and entries within this book are Westminster Abbey, the Houses of Parliament, the Bank of England, St Paul's Cathedral and the Tower of London.

TRAVEL AND GUIDED ROUTES

London is one of the most accessible cities in the world and its central area, on which the majority of this book focuses, is relatively small. Getting around is easily done via the Underground network, buses, trains, bicycle or on foot. This section gives some guidance to those options. Also included are a selection of shorter walking and longer cycling routes (using the Barclays Cycle Hire scheme), which will take you round many of the places mentioned.

The London Underground

London's Underground train network is an excellent way of getting around the city. With a Tube map in hand it is actually very difficult to get lost and going in the wrong direction is the worst that can really happen.

Single tickets, return tickets and daily travel cards can all be purchased, but the better, and cheaper, alternative is to get an Oyster Card, which you pre-load with money and is purchased from Underground stations or shops. Simply touch it to the yellow circles to open the barriers and the fare will automatically be calculated for the distance travelled and deducted. The Oyster Card can also be used to travel on some overland train journeys and London buses.

One thing to remember when using the Underground is that it is rarely worth the effort of going down to the trains to use them for one or two stops. It is often as easy and quicker to walk between the stops. For example, many people will go to Charing Cross and change at Leicester Square to get to Covent Garden when it is at most a five-minute walk above ground.

One downside of the Underground is that it can be extremely hot in the summer, especially as it is used by the vast majority of visitors to London, and it is advised to carry a bottle of water. But, in many cases, the station platforms have barely changed since the war so it is possible to get a feeling of what shelterers might have experienced during the Blitz.

Buses

London has hundreds of buses which can get you to almost any part of the city, usually within a few hundred yards of where you need to be. Bus stops are clearly marked and show the routes all buses passing that stop take.

You may be required to buy a ticket before getting on the bus from machines located next to the bus stop, but these are being phased out and you may be able to pay on board. However, as with the Underground, the Oyster Card is the most convenient and cost-effective way of paying.

A double-decker bus ride around London will, if nothing else, give an entirely different view of the city.

Trains

London is served by several mainline stations which can be found in the heart of the city. Coming into Waterloo in the south will give easy access to the entries in the Southwark, Lambeth & Wandsworth chapter, and Charing Cross is only a short walk from Whitehall and St James's Park. Marylebone station is only a few minutes' walk from the beginning of the SOE-dominated Baker Street. King's Cross and Euston are only a short distance from the City of London by bike or Tube.

The Docklands Light Railway (DLR), as the name suggests, can be used to get around the Docklands area and extends as far west as the Bank of England.

Barclays Cycle Hire

London's bicycle hire scheme is one of the quickest and cheapest ways to get around London. With hundreds of docking stations dotted around London, a bike, or a dock to return your bike too, are never far away.

It costs only £2 for twenty-four hours' access and you can use the bikes as many times as you want, although you will be charged extra for journeys lasting more than thirty minutes. Simply insert your credit card into the terminal to receive a printed code, which can be entered into a dock to release a bike.

When you are finished just return the bike to an empty dock, but do make sure the green light comes on before walking away. If the green light has not come on then the bike may not have been docked correctly and it is possible you will start being charged. If a docking station is full and you find you are running out of time, you can get an extra fifteen minutes to find another docking station, just go to the terminal and follow the on-screen instructions. The free phone app is excellent and well worth downloading. It shows the location of docking stations as well as the number of bikes and free spaces at any given time.

The only other things to remember are: if a red light is showing at a docking station then you will not be able to release that bike, and if the bike's saddle is down as low as it can go and facing backwards, this is the unofficial sign that there is something wrong with that bike.

Cycling in London is a fun and safe way to see the city, provided you obey the rules of the road and pay attention to what is happening. It is advisable to wear something highly visible such as fluorescent armbands and a helmet, although neither is provided.

In general the traffic in London does not move very fast, especially if you stay to the smaller side streets, and it is often better to avoid the bigger roads such as the Marylebone/Euston Road and Oxford Street. It is often safest to ride in the middle of the lane, or at least 1m from the pavement. Indicate your intentions with arm signals and do not be tempted to undertake vehicles (that is, pass them on the pavement side), as many accidents happen when a car turns left, not realising that a cyclist is coming through.

Finally, keep your finger on the bell and be prepared to use it to alert the pedestrians who do not look before crossing the road.

Taxis

London cabbies pride themselves on being the best in the world and will get you to wherever you want to go as quickly as traffic allows. However, they are expensive, even for a short journey.

All taxis are very distinctive (although not all are black cabs anymore thanks to a huge range of advertising). Cash is the preferred way to pay, but increasingly more cabs accept credit and debit cards, though it is best to check before you get in to make sure cards will be accepted.

If it is raining, or you are lost, or just want a ride in a London cab, stand at the side of the road and flag one down.

Walking

The most important thing to remember about central London is that it is relatively small. Many visitors to London use the Underground by default to get about, but a good map and a five- or ten-minute walk will often prove much easier and often quicker as it is a long way down to some of the platforms.

Much more of the city can be seen by staying above ground, and fantastic buildings, quirky side streets, curious shops and pubs will not be bypassed, not to mention the money that can be saved. The suggested walks will take you around some of the best sightseeing areas covered in this guide.

GUIDED ROUTES

Walking Routes

Walking Route 1: Whitehall

No visit to London would be complete without a walk around Whitehall and the government offices found there.

Starting at the Trafalgar Square end, head down Whitehall on the left-hand side pavement. Keep going for a few hundred yards until you come to Whitehall Place on the left; on the opposite side of the road you can see Admiralty House where Churchill lived when First Lord of the Admiralty. Take this left down Whitehall Place so you have the Old War Office on your right. When you get to the end of the Old War Office building there will be a right turn into Whitehall Court, where you will see the Royal Tank Regiment Memorial on the corner. Turn round and look over the other side of Whitehall Place and you'll see the Corinthia Hotel which was known as the Metropole Building, an extension of the War Office during the war.

Walk down Whitehall Court, at the end of which you will be opposite the MoD main building. Turn right past the Gurkha Memorial and up Horse Guards Avenue back towards Whitehall. You will now have the Old War Office on your right and will be opposite the Whitehall entrance to Horse Guards Parade, where you are likely to see some of the queen's Life Guards on duty. Turn left and walk down Whitehall; soon you will pass statues of Slim, Alanbrooke and Montgomery, while on your right, in the middle of the road, there is the memorial to the women of the Second World War and the Cenotaph.

Now is a good time to cross over and, if you want a closer look, go back up to see the guards on duty. If you continue down Whitehall you will soon come to Downing Street on your right, marked by the black gates and scores of policemen protecting it.

Keep heading down Whitehall past the Foreign and Commonwealth Office and take a right down King Charles Street. This narrows to a flight of steps at the St James's Park end, at the bottom of which is the entrance to the Churchill War Rooms. Take a right up Horse Guards Parade, past the statue of Mountbatten on your right and then walk into Horse Guards Parade itself. To the right (on the Whitehall side) you will see the entrance to the Horse Guards Museum, while looking straight up you'll see the back of the Old Admiralty Building and its creeper-covered bunker on the left.

Walk up past and round the bunker, bearing right, looking up to see the loopholes and machine-gun slits, and on to Spring Gardens with the front of the Old Admiralty Building on your right. At the end of Spring Gardens, take a left and head up to Admiralty Arch and back around to Trafalgar Square towards your right.

Walking Route 2: St James's North

A walk along the northern side of St James's Park will take you past a memorial to King George VI, the German Embassy, several clubs, SHAEF Headquarters, buildings used by the intelligence services and a royal palace. That has got to be worth an hour of anyone's time!

A good place to start this walk is on the Mall in front of the King George VI Memorial, with its newer addition of Elizabeth, the Queen Mother, and bronze friezes that are well worth a closer look. Once done, head up the steps past the memorial into Carlton Gardens. You can walk round the loop either way, but take a moment to look at the statue of de Gaulle at the top and then look at the building on the corner (to the right of the King George VI statue); this was the Free French HQ during the war and is marked by several plaques. As you walk along Carlton Gardens it changes into Carlton House Terrace. Just past Waterloo Place (and the handy bike rack if you cycle down) you will see No. 10, the old German Embassy.

Walk up Waterloo Place then turn left on to Pall Mall. After a short distance you will be able to take a right to get on to St James's Square. You will enter the square at the south-east corner and come upon Norfolk House, a brick building on your right, SHAEF HQ, which is marked by two plaques.

Walk along the bottom of the square and towards the Army & Navy Club, the address of which was used in Operation Mincemeat. Turn left then right, back on to Pall Mall. Keep an eye out on your right for No. 53, the old Wilkinson Sword offices, before you come to St James's Palace. You should see a pair of Foot Guards on duty at the entrance to the palace, where you can get a cheeky photo (it is always fun to see how close children dare to get to the soldiers, gradually shuffling closer). Turn right and you can walk up St James's Street. As you walk up the street you will see Ryder Street on your right, home of the SIS counter-intelligence department, closely followed by Boodle's and then No. 58 on your left, MI5's Second World War London office.

The walk ends here, but you can carry on up to Piccadilly and take a left to go past the Ritz and on towards Green Park and the Underground station by the same name. Go into the park itself to see the memorials there and in particular the impressive Bomber Command Memorial. Or you can turn right at the top of St James's Street to get to Piccadilly Circus.

Walking Route 3: Little America

The area around Grosvenor Square was so inundated with Americans during the war that it became known as 'Little America' or 'Eisenhowerplatz'. There is still a very strong American presence in the area with the massive US Embassy which overlooks Grosvenor Square. The square itself contains memorials to Roosevelt and the American-manned Eagle squadrons of the RAF, while just outside the square itself there is a statue of Eisenhower.

This walk starts on Maddox Street, which is just off Regent Street, not far from Oxford Circus and opposite the famous department store Liberty, and takes you all the way to Hyde Park. This can easily be done in reverse if you find yourself in Hyde Park.

Start walking down Maddox Street until you cross New Bond Street where it changes into Grosvenor Street; a few hundred yards along on your left you will pass No. 70, where the first overseas branch of the Office of Strategic Studies was during the Second World War.

Take the right down Davies Street, at the end of which you will be walking past Claridge's Hotel; look to your right and you will see the main entrance well marked by a plethora of very expensive cars. One of London's smartest hotels, Claridge's was home to General Marshall, the Chief of Staff of the US Army's temporary HQ in 1942 and birth place of Crown Prince Alexander Karadjordjevic in Suite 212 amongst other things.

Turn left and head down Brook Street towards Grosvenor Square; turn left on to the square and you will pass the buildings that the Lend-Lease mission used and the old US Embassy on the corner (now the Canadian Consulate). If you want, you can keep going down Carlos Place where you'll soon come across another of London's finest hotels, the Connaught, where de Gaulle was often found (if you do this, head back up to Grosvenor Square). Turn right and cross the road, and you can enter the gardens themselves via a gate on the corner opposite the Canadian Consulate; once you get to the centre you will have the Eagle Squadron Memorial on your left and Roosevelt on your right.

Take the exit behind the Eagle Squadron Memorial and turn right; walk along the bottom of the gardens and turn right and walk along the front of the US Embassy until you reach the Eisenhower statue. Behind Eisenhower is 20 Grosvenor Square, his Second World War HQ, which is marked by a blue plaque.

Turn left off the square and walk along Upper Brook Street until you come to Park Lane. You will now be able to see the Animals in War Memorial in the centre of Park Lane and Hyde Park the other side. This is the end of the walk and you can either use the crossing to get into Hyde Park, take a left to walk down to the Dorchester or take a right to get back up to Marble Arch and Oxford Street.

Cycling Routes

If you are going to attempt one of the cycling routes, do make sure you follow all the rules of the road. This information was correct at the time of publication, but road systems can change. If you find yourself faced with a one-way street it is fine to get off and push.

Cycling Route 1: Baker Street

Buildings on and around Baker Street have the most intriguing wartime past as, unbeknown to most people at the time, operations of espionage and sabotage across enemy territories were being planned.

Start at Dorset Square (a short walk from Baker Street Underground station) and, if you do not already have a bike, collect one from the rack there.

The first place of interest is 1 Dorset Square, location of SOE's RF Section. From here you will actually have to cycle anticlockwise around the square to take a right on to Melcombe Place. Take the second left on to Great Central Street and past the Grand Central Hotel, where Airey Neave was interviewed by MI9 after his escape from Germany.

Once in front of the hotel you are best off pushing the bike over the crossing and then left along Marylebone Road for a short distance until you come to Upper Montagu Street, where you can get back on the bike and start riding south. Take a left on to Crawford Street and ride on until you get to Montagu Mansions on your right, one of the many buildings SOE operations expanded into.

Keep going along Crawford Street for a few metres more to Baker Street. Take a right and you will soon come across No. 83 on your right then No. 64, just after the next junction, on your left (the latter is marked by a green plaque).

Keep on down Baker Street until you come to Portman Square, around half a mile and on your left. Opposite the square is Orchard Court from where SOE agents were dispatched to France. Keep on going and you will soon have

Selfridges on your left, which was badly bombed in the war. Go over Oxford Street on to North Audley Street and you'll soon come across a bike rack on your right.

And that's the end of the ride; time perhaps to head into Selfridges for some champagne and oysters or maybe just a coffee on Oxford Street?

Cycling Route 2: Bank to Aldwych

This is a longer ride taking in a large part of London, but the rewards are great as the route takes you from the Bank of England all the way to St Clement Danes, church of the RAF. Do not rush this route! Allowing a leisurely couple of hours to complete this ride will give you plenty of time to stop and look around.

Get a Tube to Bank, which is on several lines, and have a look at the impressive Bank of England building while heading down Bartholomew Lane (the Bank of England Museum entrance is also on this street). To the right-hand side of the main entrance is a bike rack.

Go along Lothbuy (behind the bank), on to Gresham Street and take the second left after Princes Street (where the bank of the Free French was based) on to Ironmonger Lane (this helps avoid the busy Bank junction). At the end of Ironmonger Lane take a right on to Cheapside and keep going until you see St Paul's on your left. Have a good look round the cathedral and be sure to find the Fire Fighters Memorial on the south side. There is a bike rack on the junction of Godliman and Knightrider streets to the south if you want to dock your bike and take a bit more time round the cathedral.

Pick up a bike again and carry on along Cheapside. This is the longest part of the ride as Cheapside turns into Newgate Street. At the end of Newgate Street follow the well-marked cycle signs over Holborn Circus to get to the High Holborn Kingsway Junction, where you turn left on to Kingsway. At this point it is worth getting off the bike and pushing it though the alleyway just after the entrance to Holborn Underground station and into Lincoln's Inn Fields. This is a fabulous, and surprising, London setting where you will find the Canadian Air Force building and memorial. Go round the field and turn right back on to Kingsway and ride down to the top of Aldwych. Go left round Aldwych and you will soon come across St Clement Danes church. It is worth hopping off the bike here to see the statues of Harris and Dowding, as well as to have a look at the church of the RAF (there is a bike rack in front of the church on the Strand and now is a good time to dock up). From the church walk down the Strand and take a left down Surrey Street, where you will see the entrance to the now disused Aldwych Underground station.

You can now head down the Strand, either on foot or by bike, to the junction in front of Waterloo Bridge. You could take a right up Wellington Street where you will find the London Transport Museum (handily there is a bike rack right behind it on Tavistock Street if you take the second left). Alternatively, you can carry on along the Strand, past the Savoy on your left, and keep going to get to Trafalgar Square (if you are still on a bike, you can dock it at the rack to the right of Charing Cross station). From here you are then only a two-minute walk from Whitehall and St James's.

REFERENCES

A wide range of resources have been used in the research of this book, from short histories on hotel websites, to photographic and video evidence, as well as a whole range of literature of which the following is a selected bibliography of general sources:

Bailey, Roderick, *Forgotten Voices of the Secret War* (Ebury Press, 2008)

Beevor, Antony, *The Second World War* (Weidenfeld & Nicolson, 2012)

Churchill, Winston S., *The Second World War* (The Reprint Society, 1951)

Guderian, Heinz, *Achtung-Panzer!: The Development of Tank Warfare* (Cassell, 1992)

Holland, James, *The Battle of Britain: Five Months that Changed History, May–October 1940* (Bantam Press, 2010)

McLynn, Frank, *The Burma Campaign: Disaster into Triumph* (Vintage Books, 2011)

Parker, Matthew, *Monte Cassino* (Headline, 2004)

Pile, General Sir Frederick, *Ack-Ack: Britain's Defence Against Air Attack in the Second World War* (George G. Harrap, 1949)

Rankin, Nicholas, *Churchill's Wizards: The British Genius for Deception 1914–1945* (Bloomsbury, 2009)

Sebag-Montefiore, Hugh, *Dunkirk: Fight to the Last Man* (Viking, 2006)

Strachan, Hew, *Arnhem 1944* (Tempus, 2004)

Sweet, Matthew, *The West End Front* (Bloomsbury, 2011)

Welchman, Gordon, *The Hut Six Story* (M. & M. Baldwin, 1997)

The following details more specific sources used for individual entries found in the book.

1 Kensington

Andrew, Christopher, *The Defence of the Realm: The Authorized History of MI5* (Allen Lane, 2009)

Boyce, Frederic & Everett, Douglas, *SOE the Scientific Secrets* (Sutton Publishing, 2004)

Cobain, Ian, *Cruel Britannia: A Secret History of Torture* (Portobello, 2012)

Jeffery, Keith, *MI6: The Secret History of the Secret Intelligence Service 1909–1949* (Bloomsbury, 2010)

Letter of complaint from SS captain Fritz Knoechlein

Lunde, Henrik O., *Hitler's Pre-emptive War: The Battle for Norway, 1940* (Casemate, 2009)

McGilvray, Evan, *A Military Government in Exile: The Polish Government in Exile 1939–1945, A Study of Discontent* (Helion & Company Ltd, 2010)

www.bletchleypark.org.uk/content/museum/tour7.rhtm

www.mi5.gov.uk/home.html

www.norway.org.uk/ARKIV/Other/news/greenplaque/

www.rusemblon.org/history/

2 Belgravia

Beevor, Antony, *The Second World War* (Weidenfeld & Nicolson, 2012)

Hough, Richard, *Mountbatten: Hero of our Time* (Book Club Associates, 1980)

Mortimer, Gavin, *The Blitz: An Illustrated History* (Osprey, 2010)

Rankin, Nicholas, *Ian Flemings Commandos: The Story of 30 Assault Unit in WWII* (Faber & Faber, 1998)

Vickers, Hugo, *Elizabeth, The Queen Mother* (Random House, 2005)

www.britishpathe.com/video/hyde-park-bombed

www.claridges.co.uk/about-the-hotel/history/

www.met.police.uk/history/hyde_park.htm

www.royalparks.org.uk/parks/hyde-park/about-hyde-park/history-and-architecture

3 Marylebone

Boyce, Frederic and Everett, Douglas, *SOE: The Scientific Secrets* (Sutton Publishing, 2004)

Cobb, Matthew, *The Resistance: The French Fight against the Nazis* (Pocket Books, 2010)

Demarne, Cyril, OBE, *The London Blitz: A Fireman's Tale* (Battle of Britain Prints International Ltd, 1991)

Finkelstein, Norman H., *With Heroic Truth: The Life of Edward R. Murrow* (Authors Guild Backinprint.com, 2005)

Foot, M.R.D., *SOE: The Special Operations Executive 1940–46* (British Broadcasting Corporation, 1985)

Helm, Sarah, *A Life in Secrets: The Story of Vera Atkins and the Lost Agents of SOE* (Abacus, 2012)

Marks, Leo, *Between Silk and Cyanide* (HarperCollins, 2000)

Mears, Ray, *The Real Heroes of Telemark* (Coronet Books, 2004)

Minney, R.J., *Carve Her Name With Pride* (Armada, 1989)

Neave, Airey, *Saturday at MI9* (Pen & Sword, 2010)

Stafford, David, *Secret Agent: The True Story of the Special Operations Executive* (BBC World Wide, 2000)

http://news.bbc.co.uk/local/london/hi/people_and_places/history/newsid_8937000/8937074.stm

www.bbc.co.uk/broadcastinghouse/bh_story/bh_past.shtml

www.selfridges.com/en/StaticPage/Our+Heritage/

4 Mayfair

Eisenhower, Dwight D., *Crusade in Europe* (William Heinemann Ltd, 1948)

Olson, Lynne, *Citizens of London: The Americans who Stood with Britain in its Darkest, Finest Hour* (Random House, 2010)

Vickers, Hugo, *Elizabeth: The Queen Mother* (Random House, 2005)

http://london.usembassy.gov/rcgrsvnr.html

www.claridges.co.uk/about-the-hotel/history/

www.the-connaught.co.uk/about-the-hotel/history/

www.thedorchester.com/the-dorchester-history

5 St James's

Alexander, Marc, *A Companion to the Royal Heritage of Great Britain* (Sutton Publishing, 2005)

Andrew, Christopher, *The Defence of the Realm: The Authorized History of MI5* (Allen Lane, 2009)

Churchill, Winston S., *The Second World War, II, Their Finest Hour* (The Reprint Society, 1951)

Eisenhower, Dwight D., *Crusade in Europe* (William Heinemann Ltd, 1948)

Foot, M.R.D., *SOE: The Special Operations Executive 1940–46* (British Broadcasting Corporation, 1985)

Frayn Turner, John, *Awards of the George Cross 1940–2005* (Pen & Sword, 2006)

Jeffery, Keith, *MI6: The Official History of the Secret Intelligence Service 1909–1949* (Bloomsbury, 2010)

Macintyre, Ben, *Double Cross* (Bloomsbury, 2012)

Macintyre, Ben, *Operation Mincemeat* (Bloomsbury, 2010)

Stafford, David, *Secret Agent: The True Story of the Special Operations Executive* (BBC World Wide, 2000)

Vickers, Hugo, *Elizabeth: The Queen Mother* (Random House, 2005)

Wilkinson-Latham, Robert, *Wilkinsons and the F.S. Fighting Knife*, Second Edition (Pooley Sword, 2009)

Wright, Peter & Greengrass, Paul, *Spy Catcher: The Candid Autobiography of a Senior Intelligence Officer* (Viking, 1987)

www.army.mod.uk/chaplains/23369.aspx

www.royal.gov.uk/TheRoyalResidences/BuckinghamPalace/History.aspx

www.royal.gov.uk/theroyalresidences/stjamespalace/history.aspx

www.sis.gov.uk/our-history/buildings.html

www.therag.co.uk/

www.un.org/en/aboutun/history/saint-james.shtml

6 Whitehall & Westminster

Churchill, Winston S., *The Second World War, I, The Gathering Storm* (The Reprint Society, 1951)

Churchill, Winston S., *The Second World War, II, Their Finest Hour* (The Reprint Society, 1951)

Cowley, Richard, *A History of the British Police from its Earliest Beginnings to the Present Day* (The History Press, 2011)

Fido, Keith & Skinner, Keith, *The Official Encyclopaedia of Scotland Yard* (Virgin Books, 1999)

Holmes, Richard, *Churchill's Bunker* (Profile Books, 2009)

MoD, *The Old War Office Building: A History* (Ministry of Defence publication): www.gov.uk/government/uploads/system/uploads/attachment_data/file/49055/old_war_office_build.pdf

Neave, Airey, *Saturday at MI9* (Pen & Sword, 2010)

www.churchhouseconf.co.uk/about_church_house/history

www.fco.gov.uk/en/about-us/our-history/our-buildings/buildings-in-uk/king-charles-street/

www.hm-treasury.gov.uk/about_1hgr.htm

www.met.police.uk/history/timeline1930-1949.htm
www.parliament.uk/about/living-heritage/building/palace/architecture/
    palacestructure/bomb-damage/
www.westminster-abbey.org/our-history/war-damage

7 Regent's Park to Hackney

Golden, Jennifer, *Hackney at War* (Sutton Publishing, 1995)
Jappy, M.J., *Danger UXB* (Channel 4 Books, 2001)
Macintyre, Ben, *Operation Mincemeat* (Bloomsbury, 2010)
Murphy, Sean, *Letting the Side Down: British Traitors of the Second World
    War* (Sutton Publishing, 2006)
Owen, James, *Danger UXB: The Heroic Story of the WWII Bomb Disposal
    Teams* (Hachette UK, 2010)
www.health.hackneysociety.org/page_id__64_path__0p2p40p.aspx

8 Piccadilly to Aldwych

'London's Windmill Theatre', *Life Magazine*, Vol. 12, No. 11, 16 March
    1942
Binney, Marcus, *The Women who Lived for Danger: The Women Agents of
    SOE in the Second World War* (Coronet Books, 2002)
Clayton, Tim & Craig, Phil, *Finest Hour* (Hodder & Stoughton, 1999)
Foot, M.R.D. & Langley, J.M., *MI9: Escape and Evasion 1939–1945* (Biteback
    Publishing, 2011)
Helm, Sarah, *A Life in Secrets: The Story of Vera Atkins and the Lost Agents
    of SOE* (Abacus, 2012)
Levine, Joshua, *Forgotten Voices of the Blitz and the Battle for Britain* (Ebury
    Press, 2006)
Marks, Leo, *Between Silk and Cyanide* (HarperCollins, 2000)
Marshall, Bruce, *The White Rabbit: The Story of Wing Commander F.F.E.
    Yeo-Thomas* (Evans Brothers Ltd, 1952)
MoD, *The Old War Office Building: A History* (Ministry of Defence
    publication): www.gov.uk/government/uploads/system/uploads/
    attachment_data/file/49055/old_war_office_build.pdf
Mortimer, Gavin, *The Longest Night: Voices from the London Blitz*
    (Weidenfeld & Nicolson, 2005)
Sebag-Montefiore, Hugh, *Dunkirk: Fight to the Last Man* (Viking, 2006)
http://ukinnl.fco.gov.uk/en/about-us/working-with-netherlands/history-uk-
    nl-relations/neighbours--past

www.8northumberland.co.uk/files/history/Short-History-of-8-
    Northumberland-Avenue.pdf
www.cafedeparis.com/club/history
www.fairmont.com/savoy-london/hotelhistory/
www.theritzlondon.com/about/history-en.html

9 The City of London & Tower Hamlets

Churchill, Winston S., *The Second World War, II, Their Finest Hour* (The
    Reprint Society, 1951)
Haining, Peter, *The Flying Bomb War* (Robson Books, 2002)
Holmes, Richard, *Churchill's Bunker* (Profile Books, 2009)
Jappy, M.J., *Danger UXB* (Channel 4 Books, 2001)
McGinty, Stephen, *Camp Z: The Secret Life of Rudolf Hess* (Quercus, 2011)
Nachtstern, Moritz & Arntzen, Ragnar, *Counterfeiter: How a Norwegian Jew
    Survived the Holocaust* (Osprey, 2008)
Rule, Fiona, *London's Docklands: A History of the Lost Quarter* (Ian Allan
    Publishing, 2012)
www.bankofengland.co.uk
www.royalmintmuseum.org.uk/history/timeline/index.html
www.stpauls.co.uk/Cathedral-History

10 Southwark, Lambeth & Wandsworth

Binney, Marcus, *The Women who Lived for Danger: The Women Agents of
    SOE in the Second World War* (Coronet Books, 2002)
Demarne, Cyril, OBE, *The London Blitz: A Fireman's Tale* (Battle of Britain
    Prints International Ltd, 1991)
Helm, Sarah, *A Life in Secrets: The Story of Vera Atkins and the Lost Agents
    of SOE* (Abacus, 2012)
Minney, R.J., *Carve Her Name With Pride* (Armada, 1989)
Murphy, Sean, *Letting the Side Down: British Traitors of the Second World
    War* (Sutton Publishing, 2006)
Pateman, Rob, *Kennington's Forgotten Tragedy: An account of the air-raid
    shelter in Kennington Park and the memorial to the victims killed in
    Lambeth's worst World War II bomb incident* (The Friends of Kennington
    Park): www.vauxhallandkennington.org.uk/forgottentragedy.pdf

11 The London Underground

Duncan, Andrew, *Secret London* (New Holland, 2011)
Halliday, Stephen, *Amazing & Extraordinary London Underground Facts* (David & Charles, 2009)
Hill, Maureen, *Britain at War, Unseen Archives* (Parragon, 2002)
Mortimer, Gavin, *The Blitz: An Illustrated History* (Osprey, 2010)
www.abandonedstations.org.uk/Brompton_Road_station.html
www.bbc.co.uk/news/uk-10612599
www.bbc.co.uk/programmes/p00qw23f

12 London's Memorials

Guderian, Heinz, *Achtung-Panzer! The Development of Tank Warfare* (Cassell, 1992)
Harris, Sir Arthur, *Bomber Offensive* (Collins, 1947)
Hastings, Max, *Bomber Command* (Book Club Associates, 1980)
Holland, James, *The Battle of Britain: Five Months that Changed History May–October 1940* (Bantam Press, 2010)
McLynn, Frank, *The Burma Campaign: Disaster into Triumph* (Vintage Books, 2011)
Montgomery, Bernard, *The Memoirs of Field Marshal Montgomery* (Collins, 1958)
Moorhead, Alan, *Montgomery* (White Lion Publishers, 1973)
Olson, Lynne, *Citizens of London: The Americans who Stood with Britain in its Darkest, Finest Hour* (Random House, 2010)
Rhodes James, Robert, *A Sprit Undaunted: The Political Role of George VI* (Abacus, 1999)
Sebag-Montefiore, Hugh, *Dunkirk: Fight to the Last Man* (Viking, 2006)
Slim, William, *Field Marshal William Slim: Defeat into Victory* (Cassell, 1956)
www.royaltankregiment.com
www.whitehouse.gov/about/presidents/franklindroosevelt

Bomb damage in Leicester Square, 1940.

A barrage balloon flying close
to the houses of parliament.

Smoke rising from the Docklands area.

The scene in front of the Bank of England the Royal Exchange following bombing on the night of 11 January 1941.

INDEX

If you enjoyed this book, you may also be interested in…

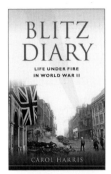

Blitz Diary: Life Under Fire in World War II

CAROL HARRIS

Blitz Diary tells the story of aerial attacks on Britain during World War Two, through the letters, diaries and memoirs of those who experienced it at first hand. Contributors include a bomb disposal expert, a housewife in the Fire Guard, a member of the WVS Queen's Messenger Convoys, as well as many ordinary Londoners. Historian Carol Harris has collected together a remarkable series of accounts from the war's darkest days, with heart-warming stories of solidarity, bravery and survival,.

978 0 7524 5172 5

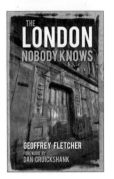

The London Nobody Knows

GEOFFREY FLETCHER

Geoffrey Fletcher's off-beat portrayal of London does not focus on the big landmarks; instead he transports you to an art nouveau pub, a Victorian music hall, a Hawksmoor church and even a public toilet where the attendant kept goldfish in the cisterns! Originally published in 1962, in 1967 *The London Nobody Knows* was turned into an acclaimed documentary film. It has been a must-have for anyone with an interest in London ever since and will surprise even those who think they know the city well today.

978 0 7524 6199 1

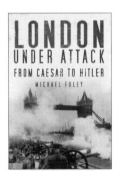

London Under Attack: From Caesar to Hitler

MICHAEL FOLEY

London has been under attack for literally centuries. This book records the dramatic military history of the capital from Roman times until the Second World War and beyond. As well as the terrible Blitz on London during the Second World War, earlier conflicts are also documented, including the Civil Wars of the twelfth and seventeenth centuries, the wars between King John and the barons, uprisings against the poll tax, the Gordon Riots and numerous other rebellions and conflicts. A must-read for all those interested in military history as well as the turbulent history of our nation's capital.

978 0 7524 5186 2

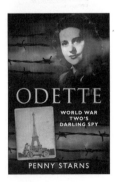

Odette: World War Two's Darling Spy

PENNY STARNS

Odette Brailly entered the nation's consciousness in the 1950s when her remarkable and romantic exploits as an SOE agent first came to light. She had been the first woman to be awarded the GC, as well as the Legion d'Honneur, but speculation about her personal life meant she soon became as controversial as she was celebrated. Historian Penny Starns delves into recently opened SOE personnel files to reveal the true story of this wartime heroine and the officer who posed as her husband.

978 0 7524 4972 2

Visit our website and discover thousands of other History Press books.

www.thehistorypress.co.uk